Daniel Gray is the author of *Extra Time, Black Boots and Football Pinks, Saturday, 3pm* and *Scribbles in the Margins*, as well as eight other books on football, politics, history and travel. His recent work has included screenwriting, presenting social history on television, editing a football magazine and writing across a number of national titles. He also presents the *When Saturday Comes* podcast.

It [football] is not a phenomenon; it is an everyday matter. There is more eccentricity in deliberately disregarding it than in devoting a life to it. It has more significance in the national character than theatre has. Its sudden withdrawal from the people would bring deeper disconsolation than to deprive them of television. The way we play the game, organise it and reward it reflects the kind of community we are.

Arthur Hopcraft in *The Football Man: People & Passions in Soccer*

Football is the most important of the least important things in life.

Arrigo Sacchi

THE SILENCE OF THE STANDS

Finding the Joy in Football's Lost Season

DANIEL GRAY

BLOOMSBURY SPORT
LONDON · OXFORD · NEW YORK · NEW DELHI · SYDNEY

Dedicated to K.G., as always x

BLOOMSBURY SPORT
Bloomsbury Publishing Plc
50 Bedford Square, London, WC1B 3DP, UK
29 Earlsfort Terrace, Dublin 2, Ireland

BLOOMSBURY, BLOOMSBURY SPORT and the Diana logo are trademarks of
Bloomsbury Publishing Plc

First published in Great Britain 2022

A catalogue record for this book is available from the British Library

Library of Congress Cataloguing-in-Publication data has been applied for

ISBN: PB: 978-1-3994-0406-8; eBook: 978-1-3994-0405-1

2 4 6 8 10 9 7 5 3 1

Typeset in Minion Pro by Deanta Global Publishing Services, Chennai, India
Printed and bound in Great Britain by CPI Group (UK) Ltd, Croydon, CR0 4YY

To find out more about our authors and books visit www.bloomsbury.com
and sign up for our newsletters

CONTENTS

INTRODUCTION

12/09/20
Jarrow 3 v 1 Durham City
Northern League Division Two

The Durham City midfielder wore the resigned look of a man trying to find a jar of harissa in Farmfoods. Up front for Jarrow, a centre-forward darted around frenetically, as if chasing a kite during a hurricane.

The referee, a woman with the air of a flustered lollipop lady, dismissed an away-team penalty appeal with a cry of 'Get up, you'. Across in one of the two small terrace sheds that resembled staff smoking areas behind a branch of Matalan, a man shouted 'Bastard' at no one in particular. I felt happier than I had in sixth months.

I was home. Not actual home, a place all of us had been confined to for long parts of the year so far, but home as in a football ground, the place where I am supposed to be. Although many stadiums across the country remained closed to supporters as they had been since March, smaller venues such as Jarrow were now permitted to admit spectators.

In the days leading up to the game, it had not been easy to find a home to go to. Positive Covid tests for players meant postponements all over the land, including in England's north-east. 'Eeee, it must be bad if they're calling off Northern League games,' a Geordie friend had said to me. 'They'd play through a nuclear holocaust, that lot.'

Imagining the footballers of West Allotment Celtic or Easington Colliery kicking around a ball made from locusts' bladders as fire raged around them was enough to cheer any Saturday morning, not that I needed cheering up. Jarrow versus Durham City, after all, was the first match I'd be attending in more than half a year. Over at last were all those Friday evenings with no fixture to anticipate and those barren Saturday afternoons with nowhere to go. Football was back. Nothing could possibly go wrong.

Newcastle Central Station had not been quite its usual self on that sainted Saturday morning. There were reassuring pillars of normality, though, the concept everyone had been talking about 'returning to' so much that no one could really remember what it meant: the epic, grandiose sweep of the station's curvaceous roof; the handsome limestone portico with its sense of occasion and arrival; and huddles of lasses laughing uproariously at a straggling member of their crew who was hobbling towards them while sipping a bottle of VK Black Cherry through a straw. All of it made my heart sing.

With a few hours to spare before kick-off, I'd taken a stroll around Newcastle, sidling up Pink Lane and then alongside the old city walls, their weathered sandstone the colour of a Caramac dropped in grit. At Chinatown, with its 14 Chinese restaurants, its Chinese supermarkets, its ornamental Chinese lantern pavement lights, its Mandarin street signs and its decorative Chinese arch, a workman broke off from talking on his mobile to ask of his companion: 'Is this Chinatown, Paul?' 'Aye,' said Paul, 'I think so, like.' Then a strange notion overcame me: I wanted to check that St James' Park, the colossal home of Newcastle United, was still there.

Checking up on football grounds had become something of a habit during the first six months of Covid's tenancy in Britain. It wasn't that I expected them to have disappeared, but seeing that a stadium was still there, looking just how it always had and *ready* for us, the supporters, when we were allowed to return, was of enormous comfort. So it was that on a summer visit to friends in Cheshire, I'd found myself surveying Stockport County's Edgeley Park, or while on a writing assignment in Glasgow diverting a walk to take in Partick Thistle's Firhill. Now I could see that the

St James' temple still brooded over western Newcastle, the second totem of this fine city after the Tyne Bridge, as if the two were bookends and its streets the stories in between. I felt reassured and may even have sighed – happily, because St James' presence whispered of a future that would one day come, and sadly because a stadium should never gather dust. On the walk back to the station for my Metro train to Jarrow, I sank deep into thoughts of the moment in March 2020 when football disappeared, and of the void that followed.

*   *   *

Our sport was everywhere and then it was nowhere. On the Thursday we talked of play-offs and calf strains. By the Friday, football had been shushed. Via a few necessarily cold press releases Saturday plans were cancelled and the right to cheer or barrack revoked. Here was an act of larceny that we absorbed and agreed with, as if a benevolent burglar were taking away a prized possession for our own good. All we could do was sigh, look to the floor and mutter 'I understand, I understand' over and over, like a schoolchild being scolded.

Come Saturday, we pondered the empty stadiums with their quarantined goalmouths. We thought of majestic old Cappielow, wind roaming unchallenged along its terraces. We thought of homely Fratton Park, a screaming banshee of a ground now quieter than a Sunday on the moon. Of course, these places are empty and silent most of the time, yet this was a starving kind of gap and a denser, more potent quiet. It was different. Games were supposed to be happening right there, right then. Now, we did not know when they would take place, if at all.

We thought too of those grounds' surroundings: the pubs that half rely on fortnightly splurges of lager and crisps, the social clubs with their untouched buffets under cling film. Then there were the programmes, bundled, tied and going nowhere. Collectors' items, per chance? Floodlights rested their eyes and padlocks handcuffed catering hatches.

That first weekend, it was easy to spot people who were supposed to be at a game. They walked eerie streets and sat in tetchy pubs, heads down and thoughts vacant. Every now and then, they would forget themselves and habits would spur an outbreak of automatic behaviour: fingers sliding to Latest Score apps; minds wondering how Ipswich Town were getting on; a quick check in the paper to see what the Sunday 4pm fixture was. Some switched to Sky Sports News in the hope of finding Jeff Stelling announcing that Swindon had taken the lead at Oldham.

By Sunday, it seemed to sink in. Numb acceptance spread. There were no scores pages to devour, no defeats to wallow in. In the evening, there was no *Match of the Day 2*. Our scarves, we realised, were sentenced to an unhealthy term on the peg. Hymns would go unsung. And how we would miss that very act of communal singing, something most of us simply do not do elsewhere. Our therapy sessions had expired.

It was not like pre-season, with its steady course to August through transfer speculation, friendly matches and new kits. Fixtures faded from the canvas rather than appearing in fresh paint. Football had no cheery shop window note declaring 'Back in 5 minutes'. All we knew was that it would return. And when it did, hell, that first goal would feel better than it had for years.

Some weeks later, it was as if the sky knew that football had ceased. Gone for days on end were the clouds. The sun hung over us unremitting, loyal and somehow spooky. Rain was something from *before all this*, like restaurants and handshakes. Football weather, with its damp Aprils and viciously cold May Saturdays, had departed on the coat-tails of the sport itself.

Once it vanished, neighbours, acquaintances or in-laws could no longer ask how our teams were faring. Footballing small talk came now through a question asked of our partners over telephones and online portals: 'How is he coping without the football?' From some, this was heartfelt, expressed in the same concerned tone with which one might enquire about the health of a poorly pet cat. From others, scorn or a roll of the eyes could be detected, as if going without football were as inconsequential as going without eggs or compost.

But how we felt did matter. Missing football is an important, valid emotion. It did not mean that we lacked perspective or that we did not cry the same distressed tears as others during news bulletins. We supporters know how far down the list of importance football is, and very few fans wished for matches to happen again until they could be played safely, and with us there. But we should never have felt the need to apologise for the brittle moments when a piece of music or the smell of grass reminded us of matchday and what had evaporated.

The very act of going to a game matters tremendously. It matters to your routine, identity and equilibrium, and it matters to the routine, identity and equilibrium of so many thousands of others. It is making the same journey, meeting the same Saturday friends, filing along the same row past the same grumbling owners of immovable knees to take your seat, or landing in the same spot on the sacred terrace. Then, it is seeing those colours you love and letting those who wear them infuriate, exult and disappoint you all over again. Our grounds mattered in all of this too – suddenly, we were exiled from our second homes.

The suspension of the fixture list itself cut deep. No longer did we have those etchings in the diary of where we would be and how we would probably be feeling in a fortnight or two months' time. The future had been erased, and with it anticipation, excitement, trains to book, something to look forward to... all the things that make being a football fan – and a human – worthwhile and occasionally joyous. Even when professional football returned three months later, to most of us it was only on television screens and jumpy live feeds. There were fixtures, but if we weren't there then they were not worth writing down. Did any of it even matter anymore? We could barely remember who our team was playing next. All of those small thrills that amass to make match-going a monumental facet of our lives crumbled away. We found morsels where we could – old highlights online, nostalgic reading, programme collection filing, stumbling upon kickabouts in the park – but the vacuum was immense.

Then in late summer, after much talk of phases, stages and steps, permission was granted for some turnstiles to be jump-started into life. Most of these matches with fans present would take place in England's lower leagues. Even then, there remained the constant threat of Covid-related postponements and the chance of sudden rule changes that would exile some supporters once more. Football was available again, but it had become hard to track down, a kind of prohibition pursuit where grounds were speakeasies and Bovril was our moonshine.

So it was that I found myself on that Metro train as it clacked over the River Tyne and towards the old shipyard town of Jarrow. There and then, I decided I would spend the remainder of the 2020/21 season trying to attend as many matches as I could, and then writing about what I encountered – stories from the seldom seen season. There would be fits and starts, and whole scrapyards of false hope.

This felt like a season that should be recorded, both in its grim hopelessness and those tiny glimmers of light that could occasionally be discerned. Though a period no one could ever wish to repeat, it was unarguably a historic one. As football is part of our national fabric and social history, its existence during the time of Covid was deserving of charting and reporting, not least because so few saw it happen. It was intriguing, too, to measure how it adapted and how supporters' feelings changed – would the love shine through with absence making the heart grow fonder, would people simply abandon the game if they couldn't physically be there in stadiums, would their exclusion alter the way matches themselves were played? If this heaviest of clouds ever shifted, would we find that the same sport emerged, its charms and eccentricities maintained? And what might we lose along the way? Never had already impoverished clubs faced greater peril.

Other motivations sat alongside that urge to observe football in its strangest time and relay what I saw. Some were universal, some were personal, and many flowed from that period when we were bereft of football altogether. I missed the promise and intrigue of travel, the being at a train station on a Saturday morning, the hearing 'goodbye' in one accent and 'hello' in an entirely different one. I missed the nuances that set towns apart, their local newspaper fonts and names for bread rolls. I missed turning a corner and seeing a new ground for the first time. In a time of dogma, few grey areas and trenchant opinion, I missed the uncertainty of a match beginning at 0-0 and being able to swing in any conceivable direction, beautiful in its unpredictability and irrationality. Conversely, I missed the certainty of the fixture list – during a period when it felt as if no one really knew what they were doing and when 'all this' would end, its firm dates, kick-off times and venues were badly needed. When schedules to follow were eventually released, it gave the secure childhood feeling of being scooped up and hoisted on to your dad's shoulders.

Throughout this time, we all found ourselves pursuing that idea of 'normality'. It seems clear now, many months on, that my travels in search of terraces were a way of chasing routine and calm. We all have our ways of coping; it is just that for some of us, this involves boarding a train for Workington. I may one day look back and see these travels as the harbinger or fulcrum of a midlife crisis – in December 2020, I entered the last year of my thirties. It was, too, a decade since I'd travelled across England for my book *Hatters, Railwaymen and Knitters*.

In the end, further lockdown and season curtailment restricted my movements: this time, my Saturdays could take me only to northern England and to behind-closed-doors games in Scotland. I had planned to work my way south as the season progressed, but that which seemed plausible in the autumn of 2020 was rendered impossible by early 2021. Grounds stayed shut or were closed again after briefly reawakening. Leagues were abandoned. I resolved to consume football whenever and wherever possible – there could be no strategy or finely-tuned balance in a year such as this one. What follows, then, is a snapshot of our national game through an abnormal period from September 2020 to May 2021, but one that hopefully offers universal stories and themes.

The continued ban – with occasional exceptions – on supporters at professional football matches also meant that most fixtures I saw took place at a non-league level. All of these constraints did not stop this sport – and its places – having stories to tell, from Kirkcaldy to Kendal. At Jarrow, my march in search of the seldom seen season began.

* * *

Reaching Jarrow's Perth Green ground meant a walk through the Scotch Estate. Referring to that name in leafier parts of Tyneside elicits the screwing up of eyes, the making of an empty whistling sound through pursed lips and a comment such as 'You're taking your life into your own hands there' or 'If you go inside anyone's house, remember to wipe your feet on the way out'. Perhaps it was the relaxed air that streets named Skye Grove and Arran Drive offered, but the most threatening thing I encountered was an odd garden sculpture on Inverness Road. It depicted a dog's rear end and was very detailed. The porcelain canine was, I think, supposed to be digging a hole, hence its decapitated appearance.

Otherwise, the Scotch Estate seemed to have lapsed into a pleasant coma, where its neatly kept gardens could be admired and its tattier efforts tutted at – and what is travel for, if not admiration and tutting? – without the risk of passing another human being. Beyond dog ornaments and homemade rainbow posters applauding the NHS in felt-tip flamboyance, it looked almost as it must have in post-war promotional plans and photographs. There was a solidity to it, perhaps reflected in the main pub's name, The Red Hackle, which sounded either like an animal you wouldn't mess with or a cough peculiar to miners. Its landlord, Lee Hughes, had emerged as a local hero during lockdown. With his pub closed, Hughes opened a community kitchen providing thousands of meals to elderly and vulnerable locals. So shines a good deed in a weary world.

Faint tannoy sounds dragged me towards Perth Green. No football supporter is able to stand within earshot of tinny pop beats and team line-up bulletins without moving nearer. We are hauled towards turnstiles, towed by this low-quality, familiar soundtrack. We are weaker than coins near magnets. I recalled a brief moment during football's absence when I realised how much I longed for this pale, crackly din. We were walking (oh the endless family walks…) by a car showroom when a breeze carried over Dario G's 'Carnaval de Paris' from its forecourt speakers. That being a staple tune of stadiums across the land was one thing, but it was the shelly, almost imperceptible outdoor delivery so reminiscent of a football ground's that trembled my lip and made soreness creep up my throat like lava. My daughter singing along 'We are the Boro/We are the Boro/We are the Boro red army' – a chant she'd learned since beginning to accompany me to Middlesbrough matches – both helped the situation and made it a thousand times worse. And to think that I don't even like that record.

Jarrow's version inhaled us through the grounds of the community centre and school with which the club share their home. It was far from the traditional stadium I'd walked towards in so many daydreams about the grand return. I quickly found it didn't matter. By this point, anywhere, any*thing* would do, and now a welcome scent of fried onions floated over us returning pilgrims. It mingled with newly cut grass and was chaperoned by the heavenly reverberations of footballs being struck as the players warmed up.

Besides, charm can be perceived in most grounds at this level of the game: what could be gentler than paying the entrance fee of £5 at an adapted garden shed, its door sawn in half to make a stable-style hatch? This was the calm, almost bucolic reintroduction to matches we all needed; anything boisterous following half a year of hermitage living may have been overwhelming. 'HA'WAY JARRA,' barked a man who clearly disagreed into my ear. If nothing else, it was a reminder that in terms of pronunciation, the 'o' and 'w' in 'Jarrow' go missing and are replaced with an 'a' somewhere near Gateshead, and then are not heard again until Sunderland.

Over by the pitch, a spectator offered his analysis of the warm-up: 'Eeee Liam, ah can see ye've not bothered fucking practising in the last six months. Bloody useless, man.' I hoped that the spectator was not Liam's father and reflected how, when supporters did start attending football again on a larger scale, it was likely to take some of them only minutes to start barracking their beloved, much-missed teams. That takes a special kind of affection.

My own affection presented itself in goosebumps. It was the blazing lime green of the pitch that did it. In all of those wasted thoughts of withheld football, I had not once considered the very turf on which the game is played, and yet its shade and scale are what kidnaps the supporter at his or her first match and never releases them. Now, its glow transfixed me and held my eyes once more. This sport's ability to return us to childhood remained intact.

It was a Saturday, at 3 o'clock in the afternoon, and I was at a football match. The old routine that had been so abruptly expunged had finally been restored. Here we were, a few hundred people feeling the same, leaning on concrete and scaffold railings in positions that one only really encounters on a terrace or, as in this case, pitchside. In the moments before kick-off, I took it all in, half convinced that the players and spectators would suddenly fade to nothing and disappear as if in some grisly fairground mirror trick.

At two-metre intervals on the opposite touchline were a dozen red velvet function suite chairs with golden frames, to be used by coaches and substitutes. Covid regulations had contrived to add something even more surreal to the already blessedly eccentric world of non-league dugouts. It seemed a shame that the club had not used a frilly chair dress with an enlarged ribbon bow, as is the custom with such furniture at weddings. Behind one goal, a bright blue Union Jack proclaimed JARRA LASSES. Beyond the wooden fence at the opposite end, teenage lads tore around scrubland on scramble bikes, entry number 27 in the *i-SPY North-East England* book.

A cloud crept away from the sun and the lollipop lady in black peeped her whistle. Durham kicked off and I became immediately transfixed by their shirts. It looked as if they were wearing flags, which they essentially were – their tops were replicas of the black, red and white standard of the City of Durham. Its red and white cross intersected in the breast area and made the players look as if they were strapped on to something, perhaps a lorry in a World's Strongest Man heat. I wondered if this might become a trend, not just with flags but other local landmarks and historical eras, so that York City might start wearing Roman-style togas or Grimsby Town those yellow oilskin macs and hats from old Fisherman's Friend tins.

Perhaps feeling a little left out, the Durham goalkeeper had made his own show by wearing fluorescent gloves that were the size of Spear & Jackson No.4 shovels. He looked like a toddler in his big brother's hand-me-down mittens. How long might it be before such dayglo accessories grow to cover the entire goal and begin to attract the attentions of low-flying aircraft? For Jarrow, the goalkeeper wore white boots and socks, the latter pulled up over his knees, and a short-sleeved pink top. It was the kind of outfit that makes football fans of a certain age start suffering involuntary tics and muttering things about a time when keepers didn't even wear gloves, and for protection relied only on a woolly green jumper and studs sharpened like flick knives.

The referee was accompanied by two linesmen, one of whom looked a little like Colonel Sanders of Kentucky Fried Chicken fame. After one unpopular decision, this resemblance led to a cry of 'Well, that's Finger Lickin' shite, lino'. His colleague had the brittle demeanour of Mr Burns from *The Simpsons*. Later, when they moved across the pitch for their half-time break, it was like watching two veterans of the Jarrow March finally returning home, having been waylaid in Market Harborough for 84 years.

Jarrow made an urgent start to the game. They dashed around with the energy of schoolkids told to tidy the classroom or face being kept back after the bell. Seminal in this frantic beginning was their bald-headed number 8, Lee Kerr. With both ankles strapped and strangled by reams of white tape, the centre-midfielder played a form of tenacious football from another era. Harassing and haranguing opponents, and then always impelling Jarrow forward when on the ball, Kerr had neither the precision tackles nor the patient sideways passes required of a safety-first modern midfielder. His was the job of making things happen. All he lacked was a cavernous 1970s terrace of bobble-hatted fans baying him forward. Kerr played like he wanted to prise six months of missed football into 90 minutes. He was my new favourite footballer.

While Kerr and his teammates were veterans of local teams and leagues, Durham City were pursuing a somewhat more exotic blueprint for Northern League Division Two success. In fact, even the idea of mediocrity must have possessed a certain glamorous shimmer; only the annulment of football in March had prevented the Citizens from finishing bottom of English football's tenth tier for the second successive season. Club owner Olivier Bernard, the Paris-born former Newcastle United full-back, had appointed fellow Frenchman Didier Agathe as manager and head of the club's academy. Agathe, for more than 120 games a dynamic and thrilling winger with Celtic, would leave behind his life on the island of Réunion for games at Crook, Billingham and Tow Law. This afternoon, and having lost three matches already, the Indian Ocean must have seemed further away than ever, especially when Agathe perched himself upon a cherry-red function suite chair.

Under Bernard and Agathe, Durham would blend local young talent with academy graduates from abroad. So it was that those of us present witnessed the unlikely occurrence of Bermudian international D'Andre Wainwright and Curaçao-capped Giorney Rojer kicking around a football on the Scotch Estate in Jarrow. Early in the game, a teammate, the Dutchman Quentin van Veenendaal, fell to the ground following a robust challenge. 'Get up!' bawled a young Jarrow player, leaning down into van Veenendaal's ear. 'That's not a foul, not in England. You're in England now.' Some of us in the crowd winced as much as van Veenendaal. If the Durham City experiment, and indeed the Northern League season, was to endure, then there could be tough and dark times ahead.

Soon after van Veenendaal's welcome to England, Jarrow were awarded a penalty and in disgust a visiting substitute knocked over a function suite chair. Liam McBryde tanked the spot kick against the crossbar. That had never happened during the lock-down matches he'd played in his head. The ball then lolloped around the area before Durham's ex-Netherlands under-18 international Maurice Kone fumbled his clearance. Forward Adam Lennox – one of few men on display with the stature, running style and physical aura of a footballer from higher up the chain – lashed the ball home. Though far from raucous or berserk, home supporter celebrations moved me immensely; seeing open displays of joy had become a rare thing in 2020. Being together had been suppressed and with it the jubilant emotions that can mean. Now Jarrow had scored, and I remembered what delight there could be in hearing the euphoria of complete strangers.

Such comforts of returning to the familiar became pleasantly overwhelming. For one thing, the language of football, with its cries of 'Man on!', 'Square ball!' and 'Hit it!', felt like coming home from a long trip abroad and hearing your own accent spoken in the airport. There were other contenting sounds too: the cattle stampede of studs on a hard pitch; the ball tumbling into the side netting and making a whipping, threshing sea shanty of a noise; an avuncular voice asking of his friend: 'Do you want tea or Bovril at half-time?' These sensations and satisfactions are like popping bubble wrap for us followers of football.

Kerr remained a whizzing pendulum and now Lennox played as if in a boyhood dream. Each nutmeg he attempted threaded elegantly through his opponents' legs, and each dropped shoulder left them looking at the gutter and he at the stars. It was apparent that a number of Durham's players were in possession of similar skills to Lennox, but somehow, they and their team played a fainter version of the game. On occasion it amounted to staccato football, where there seemed to be slow, languorous gaps in time when one Citizens player passed to another.

Inevitably, Durham scored an equaliser, because this sport has long refused to comply with what *should* happen. Wainwright sent Abdul Wahab – backed all afternoon by his own personal supporters' club of two men – free, Wahab circled his way around the goalkeeper and the international bright young things had their goal. Having strained to keep up with play, the Mr Burns linesman now wore the pained expression of a man who had received bad news at the cash machine, and then stood on a snail. In all the celebrations, another red chair was knocked over.

Just before half-time, Lennox rolled the ball forward and bounded free of his marker. That opponent was clearly a man who'd had the comfort-bingeing type of lockdown so familiar to many of us rather than the give-up-alcohol-and-exist-on-nothing-but-berries type of lockdown we'd seen in weekend newspaper supplements. It was like watching a capybara pursue a gazelle. The rest of the Durham defence scurried in odd directions, resembling spiders trying to escape from an empty bathtub, leaving Lennox to ease his way around the goalkeeper and score again. Soon after the restart, it was Kone's turn to chase. He got nearer. Too near. A red card, and no doubt dreams of far away as the Dutchman marched down a Perspex tunnel and towards Perth Green's school changing-room facilities. Agathe looked to the sky. It was blue but, you suspected, not as blue as Réunion's.

Those shared facilities had also made half-time a novel experience for the visiting supporter. Rather than the traditional catering vans or hatches, sustenance was provided from within the adjoining primary school's kitchen facilities. That meant a walk past the library with its lowered, miniature furniture to join a queue in the assembly hall. It was the first time I'd waited to buy my half-time drink on polished parquet flooring. The nostalgic scholarly feel was thickened by the whiff of fried food and the fact there were two children in the line behind me. 'They've got to keep that floor canny clean,' said one of them, 'or you can get Covid on yer school shoes. It happened to Liam Walker.' 'Aye, bet it did,' replied the other.

With ten minutes to go, Lennox scored again with another graceful goal. Whatever the level of football, to see someone so balletic in their movement and so able to tease and mould the ball is delightful. Just that thought, of the simple yet beautiful things that some players could do with their feet, thrilled me anew. For all I had missed the rituals of matchday, the stadiums and even the indulgent wallowing in a defeat on the long journey home from an away game, I realised that the very basics of the sport – the smell of grass, a fine header, a dexterous particle of skill – were just as important.

The sun lowered and autumn nudged summer aside. I glanced across this meadow with goals at each end and felt like everything was going to be all right.

1

12/09/20
Middlesbrough 1 v 1 Bournemouth
EFL Championship

Mum hands over a packed lunch, fixes her eyes on me and says: 'You will be careful, won't you?' It is September 2020, and yet it could easily be November 1996. That month in that year, when I was 14 years old, she relented after months of begging and allowed me to travel alone to a Middlesbrough away game. Putting me on a train bound for Derby, she had muttered the same words in the same loving tone.

Back then, the threats were many. I may miss my stop and end up in Birmingham. I could become lost in the shuttered world of a rainy Sunday in Derby. Or, hooligans – a word still clamped to football in the mid-1990s like the stench of stale tobacco on an old cushion – might make an easy target of a teenager whose only offensive weapon was a packet of pickled onion Monster Munch. Now, there existed just one danger: Covid. 'You'll not hug anyone if they score, will you?' she adds. 'Don't worry,' I reply. 'They'll not score.'

Recalling why I wanted so desperately to travel alone back in 1996 is difficult. Perhaps it was my idea of striking out as an independent person, brimming with those motivations that make slightly older teenagers take gap years before drifting home dressed in kaftans. Admittedly, my version would last only an afternoon, and the native dress I acquired amounted to a plastic rain poncho handed out by stewards to those of us in the front few rows of the Baseball Ground's away end. To ensure that insult was screeched rather than whispered, the ponchos were speckled in graphics of Derby's ram's head club crest. More likely than all that, though, I just wanted to see Middlesbrough and had no one else to go with.

It would be the first solitary game of many. Until you attend a match alone, you do not realise how few people do the same. Most drift towards the ground in duos, families or gangs. This is a social pastime, and to take part in isolation occasionally leaves you feeling like some unseen ghost watching a party in his old home. There is always a suspicion, probably unfounded, that you are being noticed and referred to with either pity or disdain, the schoolboy forced to eat his dinner on the teachers' table. And yet on that sodden Sky Ford Super Sunday in the East Midlands, I found pleasure in companionless watching, something that endures.

Going to games alone enables a level of immersion in all the trappings of matchday that is simply impossible when conversation is necessary. Surroundings can be properly consumed, sounds and smells contemplated, and supporters, in all their rituals and springy steps, observed. My preference always is to attend with friend, Dad or daughter, but that day at the Baseball Ground I learned that there is great solace in submerging oneself in football, swilling and basking in the occasion with absolutely no diversions.

Today, though, would represent an entirely new strain of watching in isolation. Four days previously, it had been announced that Middlesbrough were one of ten English league clubs permitted to allow 1,000 supporters into their games that weekend. These matches would be pilot events for the gradual reintroduction of crowds in increasing numbers across the land. It was something of a scientific experiment, seeking to prove that it was once again safe for grown men to shout 'Wanker' at a referee without fear of deathly consequences.

As Boro's Riverside Stadium has capacity for 34,000 people, acquiring a ticket became a profoundly contemporary version of the contest in *Charlie and the Chocolate Factory*. Those of us with season tickets were to access the club website at 8pm on Wednesday evening and then click furiously as tiny graphics of seats turned rapidly from green to red – available to unavailable, excitement to hurling the cordless computer mouse at the wall. Then, by some snap of fate or heavenly system glitch, a seat became mine. I had a golden ticket and after so many months apart from my dearly beloved, I would soon be seeing them play the Cherries of Bournemouth. Life – real, normal, *vital* life – felt suddenly tangible. It gave the loaded thrill of spotting the ocean on the horizon when making a day trip to the seaside, and the light-headed rush of that first blast of searing foreign air on the airport tarmac.

Sensations unfamiliar since March rippled through me: optimism, expectancy, having something familiar to look forward to. I smiled like Charlie Bucket and for a while became deaf to news-bulletin tidings of rising Covid case numbers. Therein lies the rub of football's genius – its capacity to soothe anxiety by distracting us from a ubiquitous plague, to overcome for a short while this ill wind with a gentle and warming breeze.

When Saturday morning came around, I sat alone on a train from York to Middlesbrough, an entire carriage to myself. I thought back to that first Derby trip and to other teenage solo errands in search of football – pilgrimages bound for Bury, Leicester, Coventry and Bradford, all embarked upon from that same station. Addiction to this game has long offered the side effect of distributing supporters to places they would never otherwise visit, gifting them an intimate knowledge of their own country lacking in non-followers. That many of them then proceeded to sing, from the safety of an away end, of how the town they were visiting was a 'shithole' was another matter entirely.

There was a poignant pleasure to looking out of a train window again, drifting among pointless and inane thoughts. All through the lockdown months, many of us had found it difficult to project forward to some better day, or to fall backwards into comforting memories of happier, carefree eras, as if to do so would altogether annihilate what morale and pluck we had left. All that seemed to exist was the cloying, static present. We were goldfishes, momentarily happy only at feeding time. Now, glancing over the terracotta rooftops of the handsome town of Yarm, I lost myself trying to remember who had scored Boro's first goal during a win at Notts County in 1993. Retreating into the past seemed safe once more. The thin cardboard chit marked 'Middlesbrough v AFC Bournemouth' set out on the table before me hinted that the future had also fluttered back into view.

My private carriage screeched and gurgled into Middlesbrough, its main bridges, the Newport and the Transporter, looking now like the open arms of two giant hugs. To arrive on Teesside and have familiar landmarks fix me in a flirty glance was a reminder of how much Saturday afternoons here were about returning to roots and origins, and walking streets that remembered my footprints.

Many of those streets were, I quickly saw, demoralised and desiccated. The pandemic had smashed poorer towns such as Middlesbrough clean in the teeth. Nothing could temper my joy at being there or at the gothic magnificence of the town hall, but nor were my blinkers chunky enough to stop me noticing whole rows of now abandoned shops and cafés. Economic blight had coupled itself on to the coat-tails of medical horror.

On Linthorpe Road, in some kind of apocalyptic duel, a bagpiper contested an evangelical preacher to see who could make the most hot air. It felt like the audio version of having to choose between eating a live wasps' nest or walking barefoot over a thousand plug sockets. The preacher, I noted, had refreshed his sermon to include reference to Coronavirus. 'God's angry at you all,' he yelled. 'You're all sinners, that's why He's sent Covid down to us. It is a bolt of lightning and we must pay.' 'That's Evelyn Wharton's lad, isn't it?' said an old lady passing by to her husband. 'Mind, he always did have a temper on him.'

I walked onwards to saintly Albert Park and paused for a while by its bronze statue of Brian Clough. Clough is revered and remembered in his home town. There is this prominent, dramatic statue and a plaque on his childhood home. A more ethereal remembrance of him lingers too in the way mention of his name turns eyes of a certain age wistful, and in the folk tales told by mams to sons and recounted in pubs and social clubs. Yet no one mentions another football manager from Middlesbrough who was comfortably Clough's equal. It is as if he is our *other* uncle, the outcast who fled years ago.

* * *

It takes just under half an hour to walk from Clough's house at 11 Valley Road to Don Revie's at 20 Bell Street, time enough to ponder why one son is forgotten and one acclaimed. An explanation frequently given is that Revie, unlike Clough, never turned out for his home-town club and, once retired from playing, spent his halcyon seasons as Leeds United manager. Another is the scandal and stereotype that mauled the former's reputation in the last decade or so of his life. In death, Clough has been lionised and his fellow Teessider lampooned. Novel and film *The Damned Utd* bottled and pickled that very mood. There is one clear truth in all of this: two of the world football's greatest managers flourished from working-class estates a mile and a half apart. Both should be celebrated.

The route of this Teesside safari skirts the housing estate landed on top of what was Ayresome Park, the sacred ground where so many of us first watched Boro, including Revie and Clough. These red-brick streets have changed little between their time and now. Still do old wasp-chewing women beat rugs against back-alley walls and still, from sometime in October, will you be asked by young muddy lads pushing around a mannequin of some kind: 'Penny for the Guy, mister?' On one gable end wall are two enormous faded old Esso logos, ghost signs surely seen by the eyes of young Revie and Clough. Times were tough then, and are now; in the window of a newsagent opposite, three postcards in identical handwriting, all with the same phone number at their foot, advertised a Man's Mountain Bike ('18 years no rust'), a Cordless Drill ('In perfect order') and Two Budgies ('One yellow, one white, and cage and food') for £60.

Bell Street in Middlesbrough is a stubby road of tight terraced houses. Much of the longer avenue young Revie knew was demolished to make way for the A66. Now, it is curtailed at one end by a fence obscuring that road, and at the other by a main thoroughfare, Ayresome Green Lane. Number 20 is a slender home with a single downstairs window and the same above. Standing out from its burnt-cherry companions, it is pebble-dashed, appropriately, in the grimy white of a well-worn Leeds United shirt. Behind the houses of Bell Street runs a wide back alley, identical to those accompanying every terrace row in this part of town. Now mostly gated and locked shut, such alleys once formed warrens of unofficial streets populated largely by scurrying children in their happy pursuits. In Bell Street's version, the boy Revie would play football with rolled-up offcuts of cloth. 'Even a bundle of rags can be dangerous when used by boys', he wrote in his 1955 book *Soccer's Happy Wanderer*, 'and the tinkle of breaking glass was commonplace around Bell Street.' Revie recalled how his father would scramble to repair each breakage, and how these comic strip mishaps helped curate his footballing philosophy that the ball should be played across the floor.

Donald George Revie was born in July 1927, eight years before Brian Clough. The Middlesbrough young Don knew was filthy poor. It had once hissed, thudded and belched all the grimy tunes of the Industrial Revolution. Times of making things, times of smoking chimneys meaning work for all. But then, the Depression poured through every stopped factory and down alleyways like some unseen and toxic lava. That window-fixing father, also Don, was an unemployed joiner. Young Don's mother, Margaret, worked as a washerwoman, taking in bundles of cloth from the slightly less poor. Don and his sisters, twins Joyce and

Jean, would trudge across town, mile after mile, collecting and delivering Margaret's linen.

Nearby Ayresome Park was both a promise and a warning. On the one hand, it was the red-barrel-roofed nirvana where Don's heroes played. Some days, he would wait on the corner of Bell Street for idols like George Camsell and Wilf Mannion as they walked by on the way to training. After his father had lifted him over the Ayresome turnstiles aged six, watching and playing football became Don's refuge and escape. 'The roar of the crowd at Ayresome Park can be heard quite plainly in Bell Street. I grew up with that roar', he wrote. 'I would watch the game with glistening eyes and then come home and play the match all over by myself in the back street which measured just ten feet across. Here in this enclosed space I learned the rudiments of ball control. In fading light – often until darkness fell – I would flick a ball against the wall, fasten on to the rebound, and go dribbling it around the iron gratings. In my imagination, I could hear the roar of the crowd.'

Conversely, backing on to the Holgate End, Ayresome's terrace 'kop', was a workhouse that had only recently closed and now lingered dormant, an empty threat that the direst of days could easily return. The Revies, like so many Depression-era families, were haunted by the poverty they lived through. This spectre hung over Don until his death in 1989; his perceived greed in leaving the England manager's role for a job in the United Arab Emirates can be charted directly back to what he knew as a child. When a boy has watched his father search streets and parks for twigs to burn on the fire to warm his children, the man he becomes never forgets.

Then, in 1939, when Don was 11, devastation rained down. Margaret passed away, taken by cancer. 'When she died it was the greatest tragedy of my young life,' he said. 'Only a boy who has lost his mother knows what heartache it means.' Don senior became the single, unemployed father of three, a heartbreakingly difficult task in any era, but especially through one in which war loomed and then descended. Middlesbrough, with a steel industry attractive to Luftwaffe explosives, was the first English town bombed in World War Two. As ever, Don retreated into football. Each day he would arrive at Archibald Road school – still alive and thriving in all its Victorian pomp and stature – and practise alone: 'In the dull grey mornings of winter, flicking that ball against the wall helped to pass the time. I didn't feel so lonely... I didn't miss my mother so much.'

This regime, and those back-alley Bell Street games, paid off. Having left school and become a bricklayer – a familiar fatherly plea that he 'get a trade behind him' ringing in his ears – Revie impressed while playing for an amateur side, Middlesbrough Swifts. Though it may appear geographically puzzling, the Swifts were a feeder club for Leicester City, and in the summer of 1944 Revie was signed by the Foxes. So began a career that took him to many heights and places, but he would never live on Teesside again.

While Revie left Teesside, it never left him. His accent and direct, frequently abrupt way of addressing people were traits so steeped in the region that he should have been stamped 'Made in Middlesbrough', like so many beams and rivets of iron and steel once were. There was that financial paranoia, chiselled into his being by a Boro childhood, which plagued the rest of his days. Further, Revie ascribed to this town the abundant superstitions that came to characterise his managerial reign at Elland Road. They began, he said, the day Margaret carefully guided him away from walking underneath a painter's ladder as the two walked to the shops. 'To this day', Revie would say, 'I am the most superstitious man in the world.'

So followed from that ladder dodge the same blue mohair suit and tie each season and the charms he kept in its pockets. Ditto the fear of ornamental elephants, the distaste for bird images in pictures or emblems, sitting in the same place on the team bus and in the team hotel dining room, and the way Revie would always walk the same route to the dugout, and stroll to a set of traffic lights and back before Leeds United away matches. There were more, some that involved other people: Revie's wife, Elsie, was compelled to wear the same fur-lined suede lucky coat to every game for five years, and the manager told some players which boot to put on first and where to stand in the line before running on to the pitch. Ever since his mother instructed him never to turn away any gypsy who knocked at their door on Bell Street, he had believed in their power too. Revie the player put his man-of-the-match performance in the 1956 FA Cup final down to a piece of lucky bark a gypsy had given him; Revie the manager insisted Leeds's trophy famine was caused by a Roma curse on Elland Road and had a gypsy from Blackpool work her exorcising magic on all four corners of the pitch.

Revie's proud playing career, managerial prowess and eccentric ways sprang from Bell Street. His life was mapped out on each rain-shined cobble. A titan that changed football, born and raised on this slight road in a small town and now wiped from its history. At the very least, a plaque should be raised and Middlesbrough people should talk of their other great son.

* * *

Across town, with two o'clock approaching, a couple sat on a bench beneath the Transporter Bridge. With plastic flutes of Prosecco, they toasted someone now absent from their lives. 'He loved it down here,' said the woman. 'Aye, except that time it stank of fish,' replied her partner. He then nodded in my direction, the warmest of gestures on Teesside, where government Covid instructions not to hug non-family members were roundly met with the question, 'What, people hug non-family members? Where's that, like? France or summat?'

In its chirpy blue the shade of corner shop plastic bags, the Transporter Bridge was as solidly beautiful as ever. When you are born by this part of the River Tees as I was, to gaze at it is to be greeted by a thousand smiling, avuncular faces. It seems to belong simultaneously to everyone and just to you. Today, with the sun in the right place and the Tees serene, the treat was inflated by catching sight of the bridge's double on the water's surface. A tour group sat around making sketches on pads of paper, and if it wasn't for a teenager grizzling 'Darren! Are you fucking joking us, mate?' into his mobile phone, and the heavy wails of a tugboat's foghorn, this could easily have been the Seine or the Tiber. Then a sharp burst of wind ushered over a torrent of distant public address noises from the Riverside Stadium. I moved as if my mum had just called me in on Chippy Tea Night. It was time to go back.

In my head on the train here I'd imagined them all: the hordes bounding as one towards 3pm, towards the stadium, by the long curving road and on the scrubland around the docks that lead there. There were the families, red and white kids scrambling to keep pace with dad, and the gangs of lads on the booze and cock-sure in their throaty hollers. There were old women in twos with their acrylic shopping bags bearing flasks and blankets, and young couples who had found that going to the match together was their thing. All marched towards the usual Saturday carnival and its cabaret acts: lotto sellers, sizzling burger vans, programme stalls, a man crying 'hats and scarves and pin badges, get your pin badges hats and scarves' like some chanting Gregorian monk gone rogue.

Instead, I felt more alone than I ever had before. Not one of the other 999 Charlie Buckets and Veruca Salts was walking. Indeed, the club had encouraged people to drive in and park by the stadium for the avoidance of public transport and its sociable nature. I felt as if I were in a dream where all football fans had been banished from the Earth and it was my job to find them. With the exception of two council workers handing out Boro-branded face masks, all the game-day life of this place had faded to nothing. Remove the people from LS Lowry's painting *Going to the Match*, and all you have is space and shapes.

Only memories could summon the faint outlines and ghosts of what and who should have been there. Just as a psychic medium claims to feel energies in haunted rooms, I began to convince myself that I could smell fried onions in the air. Such was the surreal, otherworldly mood, I would not have been surprised if the statues at the Riverside's entrance of two Revie heroes, George Hardwick and Wilf Mannion, had begun speaking to one another. Showing my ticket to the steward at a cordon by the car park's edge, I suddenly had that discombobulating feeling of being secretly drunk in front of a boss or parent.

Yet by the turnstiles something shifted. The uncanny atmosphere melted away and a wonderful thought sank in: I was about to enter the Riverside Stadium, a notion that for half a year of exile had made my eyes moisten, and something that in certain bleak moments I had imagined might not happen for many more months or longer. 'Welcome back, son,' said a steward by turnstile 23.

He invited me to sanitise my hands, pointing towards a container on a table. This particular liquid – and, boy, had I become an expert in recent months, from the sticky spent-match-smelling substance in Tesco to my local shopping centre's runny eau de turps – possessed a pleasing medicinal whiff not unlike Ralgex, one of football's most evocative scents. Mimicry, recall and imagination would, I realised, be important in this new scene where nothing could ever be quite as it was. We would have to be children at play, forging whole worlds from the merest hint or idea.

There were to be real and complete, fulsome thrills too, not least the heartening, nourishing rush of shoving forward the scarlet turnstile and crossing the threshold into the ground. It gave the feeling of being able to jump into a photograph from another era.

Not a soul lingered in the concourse area, its bars shuttered and workers laid off or furloughed. When football went to sleep, many jobs were put into hibernation too. This place of queues and hubbub, of moaning at the price of a rushed half-time pint, felt now like an underworld, some abandoned catacomb with hieroglyphics in the language of another time – 'Pie + Pint Deal: £5.50' and 'Parmo in a Bun: £4'. My eyes, though, were quickly beckoned towards a gangway entrance, that portal into a more splendid universe.

Up and in I went, expecting only partially numb half-feelings, given the nature of attending a game in a 1/34th-full stadium alone. Instead, happy prickles formed the minute I turned a corner and saw the emerald turf, one goosebump for each blade of grass. I was George Bailey from *It's A Wonderful Life* back in old Bedford Falls in time for Christmas: 'Hello steward, hello seat...' Even in such reduced, curtailed circumstances, the air crackled with expectancy and a sense of occasion. Noise – solo applause and cries of 'Come on the Boro', greetings flung across rows of seating to Saturday friends unseen in yonks – began to rise and hung long in the air. For the first time in what felt like an age, we had somewhere to be; our fixture anchor was once more stable in the ocean bed.

All 1,000 of us were scattered across the main stand's two tiers like counters in the early stages of a game of Connect 4. No away fans would be permitted, another first in a time of too many. There were three seats in between each supporter on a row, with those rows staggered so that no person sat in front of another. At least, for once, I would not stand out during a solo sojourn. Behind me, a family of three sat spread over several metres so that I was able to hear all Haribo requests made from son to father and learn from mum that Auntie Jean's thyroid was playing up again. To my right, an excited man in his fifties arrived and clearly had something to share. 'Here, mate,' he bawled across, 'the hot water taps are working. The hot water taps, in the Gents. That's never happened here before. There's soap as well. Soap!' The man then looked ahead to the pitch, vacantly shaking his head and visibly muttering the words 'Hot water!' and 'Soap!' as if he'd just returned from the distant future. He was not wrong either; I couldn't remember the last time I'd experienced hot water in *any* football ground toilets. Once, in the away end at Preston North End's Deepdale, I'd heard a man enter a cubicle and cry out mockingly, 'Ooooh, toilet roll. Posh!'

Below us, the familiar stretches and drills of two squads warming up unfolded. Outfield players formed circles and played piggy in the middle while goalkeepers donked enormous passes to one another. It was mesmerisingly soporific, the very and welcome opposite to watching graphs of Covid death rates on television. 'Have we gorra keep these masks on?' shouted mum from behind me as a steward passed in front of us. He was quick enough in providing an answer ('No, only in inside areas, darlin"), but then decided to stay a while. 'But don't talk to me about masks,' he said. 'The club've only given us one to last the whole season, it's bloody ridiculous.' The steward then removed that mask so that we might hear him better. 'And look at this,' he continued, pinching the material between forefinger and thumb. 'Thin as owt. I reckon Warnock's bought a job lot, me, like.'

'Warnock' was Neil Warnock, Boro's 71-year-old manager. Though a wily dealer in the transfer market, it was not clear whether he had moved into PPE procurement. Having been appointed in June, the Yorkshireman was yet to oversee a Boro game with fans in attendance, and this afternoon would not remedy that; having caught Covid, Warnock was in isolation, his team talk given via a screen installed in the dressing room.

As all the commotion that 1,000 people can make in a stand with 10,000 seats soared, the PA announcer inexplicably decided to unleash a light and sound show of bemusing ferocity. Dance music more suited to midnight at Creamfields pounded ears and spotlights flashed as if trying to coax Martians from the sky. 'Bit much this, like,' bayed dad to mum six seats away. 'You what?' she replied. The man to my right again looked at his hands, still marvelling at hot water and soap.

Just before three o'clock, this frenzy abated and the Middlesbrough team strolled on to the pitch, followed by their visitors in a kit of turquoise toothpaste colour. Two or three people began to sing 'Come on Boro/Come on Boro' and the chorus sailed groggily and steadily across the stand, as if each person was checking that they were allowed to make noise and indeed still could.

Soon, most of the choir sang, the first time they had done so together since March. On went the hymns – 'We love you Boro, we do' and all the rest – and in front I watched as four smartly dressed members of club staff smiled at one another and gave fond shoulder shrugs. Their gestures reminded me of parents catching each other's proud eyes during a child's nativity performance. Though starved of people, the stand seemed to reverberate with sound, a deep echo. It gave the woozy release of a fairground ride or telling someone you loved them for the first time. How we had missed this spontaneous, ill-tuned serenading of our team, this caterwauled expression of devotion. Here we were, singing in church again.

The game kicked off shrouded in another cavernous roar and soon Boro midfielder George Saville – a kind of cockney Roadrunner – sliced a shot towards goal. It absconded with the trajectory of wire through cheese and ended closer to the corner flag than the target. My neighbour momentarily looked away from his hands to mutter 'Load of shite, Saville man'. Those 30 seconds – the dreadful attempt on goal and that wearied admonishment – were a homecoming equal to the singing. Everything had changed and nothing had.

When the noise lulled, as it does in all matches no matter the attendance, the furious tapping of laptop keyboards could be heard, like thousands of rattling dentures, from the press area at the stand's rear. The rising and falling lawnmower intonations of commentators and reporters could also be discerned, and I imagined that this was a gladdening experience for them too after so many months of talking about games in barren stadiums.

Bournemouth, relegated last season after half a decade in the Premier League, fizzed and zipped the ball around as if to announce that they were from a different and elevated planet. David Brooks, a wispy pimpernel of a player in low-rolled socks, curved in a wily but flawed shot that many goalkeepers would have caught. Instead, the Boro custodian, Marcus Bettinelli, dived as if attempting to prevent a rock from smacking an old lady in the face and flipped the ball out for a corner. Arnaut Danjuma, a £13.7m Dutchman, lolloped over to take it before raising one arm in the air. It is always enjoyable to try and decode what a corner signal stands for, and on this occasion the answer was 'Underhit cross that fizzles out on the edge of the six-yard box'.

Boro, though, have long been experts in relighting the dead candles of other teams, and their failure to prod, hack or will the ball clear allowed Dominic Solanke, a £19m Berkshireman, to heel the ball goalwards. There, it shaved one of Marvin Johnson's knee tattoos and tumbled into the net, a squirming and trickling goal. 'You forget, don't you,' said the mum behind, 'that we're a bit shite really.'

Early in the second half, a man sneezed thunderously and one of those nearby club staff members jumped and shuddered in her seat. She then sanitised her hands and offered a worried look to her colleagues. Distract it might, and even send us momentarily into bliss, but football was not hermetically sealed from the fears that stalked every other waking moment. Nonetheless, this stupendous sneeze seemed to scare Boro into life, a starting gun or a distress flare. They found a vivacity completely absent from the first half, as if they had left the pitch as caterpillars and returned as butterflies. Passes were suddenly streamlined and masterly, tackles bullish and precise, and efforts on goal a pleasure rather than a chore. Jonny Howson, who had used lockdown to cultivate a dashing mane of hair that flopped around like a cheerleader's pompom, became imperious in midfield, while Northern Irishman Paddy McNair seemed suddenly stronger than every other player on the field, a tank among prams.

Those actions roused the crowd, as did a sequence of fouls by the Bournemouth wing-back Jack Stacey, each worse than the last, as if he were a boxer building up to a knockout punch. It was not to come; the Cherries withdrew Stacey before the referee did it for them. Prior even to the raising of the substitution board, a sonorous voice coming from somewhere behind me – possibly Darlington – bellowed 'Number 17, yer going off, we all bloody know it', and I rejoiced at the Colosseum democracy of the football ground.

With ten minutes to play, there came a moment we had waited for through all those silent Saturdays and anxious bulletins.

McNair took custody of the ball close to the right-hand touch-line, 50 yards from goal. With an elegant sweep of his right foot, he sculpted a cross that arced into the box like a finely cast fishing line. It conjured its way over a flummoxed and befuddled Bournemouth defence and on to the head of leaping Marcus Browne. A goal, 1-1. Cue an eruption of the kind previously thought impossible among so few sparingly distributed humans, the din of a thousand lockdowns escaping from lungs. It was a cheer that returned us to hedonism and being in the moment. We did not want to be anywhere else on Earth. Heads dizzied and eyes watered. It was the greatest 30 seconds in six months, and it felt like therapy.

Sung tidings of how Boro made us happy when skies were grey swept across the stand, a gust of joy. Bettinelli saved again like a thespian in gloves and the referee called time. We sang and clapped the team from the pitch and congratulated ourselves as if we were responsible for the equaliser and the result, just as it should be. From the tannoy came the scores from elsewhere and it was completely possible that we had slipped into another parallel, altogether more blissful and blithe world.

2

26/09/20
Lancaster City 1 v 2 Basford United
Northern Premier League Premier Division

The train jabbed its way through the Cumbrian countryside, rudely interrupting life in Yanwath, Whasset, Shap and other places that sounded like an ancient Viking sneezing ritual. There was a thorough, duvet-like form of comfort in looking out to the Lake District countryside and reflecting on how little it had changed in several hundred years. This exalted land had been unstinting and unaffected by all wars and weathers, and sheep knew nothing of face masks and no dale had a 10pm curfew. It looked this way when people in pubs named the Drunken Duck and the Dog and Gun fretted over Spanish flu, and would still look this way when 'Covid' was an arcane term in an old book. Autumn sun tickled mountain peaks like the ink of a giant highlighter pen. To look on was to feel reassuringly insignificant.

'EH!? You what?' snarled one of two men in their fifties who had got on at Carlisle, brothers apparently: 'Mam got her roof done without telling me? What for?' They had decided to sit at separate tables, meaning a hollered conversation that could only have been avoided by my hiding in the toilet or swallowing a cyanide pill. 'Well, it was leaking, wasn't it,' replied the other, and I suppose he had a good point. As they alighted at Oxenholme, the first brother switched topic:

'They'll get beat y'know.'

'Eh?'

'Carlisle. They'll get beat at Barrow next week.'

'What's that gorra do with Mam's roof, you little knobhead?'

'Nowt. I thought we'd finished with that.'

I suspected they wouldn't be 'finished with that' for quite some time to come. Siblings rarely are.

It was, though, enjoyable to eavesdrop on a small parcel of football conversation. As matches came to a pause or went on without us there, the chances of brief encounter 'Who've you lot got today?' conversations in railway stations were low, and lost was the bleary-eyed Monday morning recap of money spent and points dropped as office kettles simmered. Indeed, it felt sometimes as if many people did not even know that matches like that at Jarrow and today in Lancaster even existed – 'Football?' they'd ask. 'Is that even *allowed*?' It had gone from this country's most ubiquitous pastime to one of its most furtive.

In a field outside Kendal, one Friesian cow rested its head on another's back as if tired of watching trains all morning and was now pining for another view. Hoisted above the broad and lapping River Lune, we curved into Lancaster. It was a grand arrival only improved by a jolting glance of Giant Axe, the fetching venue for today's game. A groundsman forked his pitch, dreading those philistines in polyester who would later pock this pasture, and a woman raised the shutter of a catering hatch with a hook on a wooden pole. It was lunchtime on Saturday and football was stirring, just like it should.

As when glimpsing from a train window or talking about Mam's roof and Barrow versus Carlisle United, the pandemic did occasionally retreat from our minds during these purgatorial days of mild restrictions and swirling rumours of another lockdown. Then, some dark hint would offer itself up as a reminder that made our hearts thud with worry like a debt collector's knock. There were hissing, sneering devils on most shoulders. So it was in Lancaster, where wall graffiti by the railway station declared '"HERD IMMUNITY" 45k DEAD, NEVER FORGET' and a handwritten sticker claimed, somewhat more bizarrely, that '"Covid" is mutating into communism'. Seeing me pause on a bridge to read the latter, a man had shaken his head and offered: 'There really are some mad bastards around.'

The vintage streets of Lancaster offered immediate, grounded serenity. Still-dewy cobbles unfurled uphill, an industrial carpet. They landed me on Castle Park, a row of Georgian splendour, all poise and preserved gas lamps.

Opposite, Lancaster Castle loomed like an ornate warning, its limestone bricks weathered into the camouflage colours of some rare desert tortoise. By those walls, a rock waymarker the shape and shade of a mucky canine tooth wore the words 'Witches 400' on its front. It marked the 400-year anniversary of 1612, when eight women and two men from Pendle had been accused of witchcraft and hanged here. After so many months of living a predictable, patterned and geographically confined existence, in places like this I would once more have to acquaint myself with the way architectural beauty so often nuzzles sites of historical sadness. In the old towns are the worst tales.

Further down Castle Hill, a dozen or so buildings with advent calendar windows, each a different height to the next, stooped and leaned in on one another conspiratorially, leaving a narrow opening at their conclusion. There was something almost unreal about this ancient city, and a map on China Street revealed street names that seemed to be channelled through an American cine-matic view of merrie olde England: here were Horseshoe Corner and Sun Square, and there were Slip Inn Lane and Bashful Alley.

Market Street stemmed these wonderland delusions with its battalion of determined shoppers. My own reverie was snapped when a fog of vape smoke descended over me, a very modern conjuring trick. Its sickly scent resembled blackcurrant Lemsip and left me pining for the days of being caught instead in the tarry mist of a John Player Special or a Silk Cut Purple. Things were the same at football matches. There, wafts of banana, bubblegum and custard had made official stadium smoking areas smell like a local market you'd be taken to in order to eke out a package holiday day trip.

On Market Square, a busker with the look of a hungover Pep Guardiola sang Carole King's 'You've Got a Friend' to a long queue outside the City Museum. It was a lifting moment, finding 30 or 40 people – hand-in-hand couples, dads with hopping kids, gangs of women obviously on a loud and happy day out – clearly so enthralled at the idea of an hour or so's learning and quiet reflection. Except it turned out that the museum was closed and they were all lined up for their turn in TK Maxx, that jumble sale with security tags. 'What would a Roman soldier... make of Lancaster today?' posed an information board opposite. He'd be bemused by the size of the queue for TK Maxx, I thought, imagining him standing there, excitedly hoping to pick up a Wallace and Gromit toastie maker for £7.99 or a Jasper Conran shirt that'd look great during next month's invasion of Arabia.

Pep moved on to 'Love Me Do' and I sat on the broad steps of the museum and contemplated a local council Covid sign that read CONTROL IS IN YOUR HANDS. Next to me perched three men in their seventies. One rolled a cigarette, staring at it with the intensity of a cat about to pounce on a butterfly, while his friend endlessly fiddled with the rim of his knitted beanie hat. Completing the trio was a man with a regimented side parting and burgundy trousers of the type only usually seen in Kensington or Bath. He wore a surgical mask and began to speak from behind it. This led to multiple appeals of 'You what?' and 'Eh?', before Rollie imparted: 'I can't understand you with that bloody muzzle on.' After a pause, the hat fiddler replied, 'Well, I don't understand the bugger without it.' It was the closest I'd ever come to being in a scene from *Last of the Summer Wine* and it left me immensely cheerful.

I walked on, Pep's 'American Pie' fading the further away I moved. Spread around Dalton Square were the sellers of Charter

Market, a busy resident here for hundreds of years. Now, older stalls with stripy tarpaulin awning that sold CDs from plastic boxes or dog toys and phone cases were infiltrated by tiny vans and dayglo gazebos offering Street Food. In recent years, most towns had begun to offer such things or their Farmers' Market cousins. Nonetheless, 'Street Food' still sounded to me like something you picked up from the ground as a kid. Then your mum would slap it out of your hand and reprimand you for being 'a dirty little article'. Maybe she'd do the same now, should you purchase an £8 halloumi and tahini shawarma wrap. Certainly, the statue of Queen Victoria at Dalton Square's midpoint appeared to be turning her nose up at the aromas rising from the vegan beet burger kiosk.

Presiding over this contented little scene was Lancaster Town Hall, a mighty Edwardian structure designed by the architect of the Old Bailey in London. It is the kind of intimidating pile that you imagine smaller buildings cower in front of and call 'Sir'. Walking by the structure's stunning front pillars and ornate carvings, and being careful not to make eye contact with it lest it offered me inside for a fight, I reached the canal.

By this pretty spot of trees draping over sedate water, I realised that Lancaster was not some fantasia or theme park, but a model railway town, something dreamed up by a little boy with every Hornby accessory money could buy. It had its gaping river and quaint canal, its viaduct railway and citadel castle, its smart and showy houses and municipal establishments, its homely football ground and a park of the drama and scale only a child could imagine.

It was uphill towards this Eden – Williamson Park – that I walked now. In some cosmic bowing of east and west, of Tyneside and Lancashire and of shipyard and lake, or just a lack of imagination among those who make these decisions, once again I walked through streets named after Scottish places. Argyle and Elgin, Dunkeld and Perth, Dundee and Balmoral, and yet more still lined up, layers of sandstone terraces built for the workers of the adjacent Scotch Quarry.

Not far from the park, a plaque on the wall of Lancaster Royal Grammar School commemorated former pupil Richard Owen, who in 1842 'invented the term "dinosaur"', translating the phrase 'terrible lizards' into Greek to give us 'Dinosauria'. Owen was one of the great palaeontologists of his – and any – age, and founded the Natural History Museum. The *Oxford Dictionary of National Biography* refers to him as 'the most important and most influential natural scientist of his generation'. One of his scientific adversaries, Gideon Mantell, called him 'overpaid, over-praised and cursed with a jealous monopolising spirit'. Now, he has a local Wetherspoons named after him, that highest of honours, and when you google 'Richard Owen, Lancaster', one of the top hits is a Lancaster Live story headlined 'Customers "shooting from both ends" after visits to Lancaster Wetherspoons'.

Through the gates of Williamson Park, I walked behind a couple listing people they knew who were not, in their shared view, good enough at social distancing. This had now, apparently, become a character trait or personality flaw. 'Fiona? Fiona Fenton? The more you move away, the closer she gets... And her Dave. He's worse, if anything. And he offered me one of his Polos.' 'Well, what about Bill, Barbara's neighbour. By Christ, he come right up to me in Wilko's the other day, going on about coleslaw.'

On the main hill of this handsome place, a Victorian paradise above the city, families unrolled picnic blankets in defiance of the grumpy clouds above. 'It'll burn off, that,' said a dad as only a dad could. I climbed the stairs of the spectacular Ashton Monument, reassuringly visible from all parts of the city, and looked across to the lakes and mountains beyond. Around me, old ladies talked about long gone times, toddlers begged for ice cream and kids declared races with their mums. It all sounded delightful, a soundtrack of the prosaic and regular. People need these noises.

Down the hill back into town, I walked behind an old man in a zipper cardigan and flat cap, the steady clunk of his walking stick tapping on the pavement like the slow ticks of a broken grandfather clock. With his other hand he held a portable radio to his ear, and I knew he was going to the match.

*   *   *

For those of us consumed by football, there is no merrier stroll than the walk to the game. None of us strut to the shops, the railway station or even the pub with the same expectant and gullible air. Heads up and looking forward, with gallant strides we move towards the ground in a harmonised matchday pace. There are few stragglers and overtaking is rare. In no other circumstances do we trek with such shared purpose, a dishevelled marching band without its instruments.

Early on, in the town centre, we decipher our fellow travellers via far subtler clues than coloured hats and scarves. They have a gait that other wanderers do not, pulled as they are towards a three o'clock appointment with applause and grumbling; they have some place to be. In those rotten days of lockdowns and sealed turnstiles, every afternoon amble 'Just to get out of the house' felt especially aimless. Now, those turnstiles were chirping again, Sirens luring us in with their industrial lullabies.

In Lancaster, a steady infantry undertook the 2.45pm gallop towards Giant Axe. On the railway bridge, they talked of last night's curry and tonight's telly in lullaby-soft Lancastrian accents that could dissuade wasps from stinging or send rabid dogs to sleep. Their gentle tones matched their club's pleasing, sweet nickname: the Dolly Blues, deriving from a locally produced washing tablet whose colour was said to resemble the team's shirts. The somewhat less benign 'Giant Axe', meanwhile, is so named because, when viewed from above, the neighbouring wall that guards the sports and recreation grounds the stadium sits within resembles, well, an axe head. It added a false aura of intimidation to what was an amiable and hospitable place to watch football, as if a Cotswold village newsagent had decided to employ two doormen called Mental Mick and Terry Three Fingers.

We flocked towards rink-a-tink tannoy music once again, our noses seduced by the gathering vapours of fried food. At the entrance to Giant Axe, a next-game board with the rusty thin legs of an elderly ostrich advertised today's encounter with Basford United, a club from suburban Nottingham. I adore these contraptions with their permanent home-team names in bold letters and their spaces on to which visiting team details, fixture dates and kick-off times can be hooked, slid or stuck.

Across the entire land, no ground's board is the same as the next's. Each has its own size and shape, colour scheme, typefaces, varying amount of information and sponsorship logo. There is no uniform location for one, and they are scattered in car parks, on club shop walls or among overgrown grass in a corner of the ground that time and maintenance men forgot. The very best are visible from an adjacent road, so that we might encounter them on some humble Thursday afternoon and feel a frisson of excitement about a matchday yet to happen. We may merely be passing through, and the fixture advertised may be impossible for us to attend, and yet still there is a faint tingle or a pleasant moment of distraction. These are the cinematic neon NOW SHOWING displays of football.

Some next game boards offer embellishments beyond the basics of V and KO, details that tell us about club and place. This was the case with Lancaster City's, a lofty specimen in four shades of blue whose italics seemed to ask us politely to *Come and Support The Dolly Blues*. A broad white strip at the board's foot gently advised the visitor of Giant Axe's finest offerings: 'Traditional Real Ales – Draught Lager and Bitter – Dolly's Diner – Tea & Coffee, Pies & Peas, Chips & Curry'. It was a splendidly northern smorgasbord and in the mentally vulnerable, wobbly-bottom-lip world of autumn 2020, it felt like a cheerful wave from a stranger on a train. Had it mentioned gravy, I would have cried.

In the Giant Axe car park, tyres rolled over gravel and flying loose chips made the sound of cap guns being discharged. People in blue scarves smiled at one another and said things like 'I didn't know whether to bring a big coat or not. It's that kind of weather' and 'It can't make its mind up, can it?' Behind the West Road End terrace, a club office had been fashioned from a freight container. A glance into its doorway revealed a man in a flat cap, trench coat and smart suit. On his right arm he wore a khaki canvas haversack. He looked as if he'd popped by in 1943 to follow up an accusation of ration book fraud and never left.

As turnstiles rattled and ratcheted, two stewards were charged with taking supporters' temperatures via small plastic guns. Three attempts at scanning my forehead failed. 'I think that means you're technically dead,' said my own steward tester, before smacking the gun a few times on her wrist. 'Bloody thing,' she continued. 'Think club got 'em in Poundland.' In the end it showed a reading of some description ('Dickhead'?) and I was nodded through the turnstile block, another repurposed freight container, and into a corner of the Axe.

Players thumped warm-up passes across the broad and bumpy pitch and fans nodded their greetings and found their usual spots on three terraces and in their grandstand seats. Almost every wall, fence and barrier was painted in home colours, a cheerful, sentimental blue resembling that found on a school exercise book or mechanic's overalls. By the catering hatch, kids jangled pocket-money change while calculating what they could afford. The hatch had a gleaming and ample tea urn and Walker's Crisps in baskets, such a welcome and honest WRVS café ethos in a Starbucks world.

By a corner flag in north Lancashire, then, I was reacquainted with the joyously dizzy feeling of arriving to find a ground and its plotlines laid out in this manner. There is usually almost too much to take in, an excess of intrigue. I feel giddy, something I used to become embarrassed about, as if grown-up joy should be mild and caused only by work promotions or good restaurants. Now I embrace this passing exultation, which should be the case with any pastime that can chisel such emotions from the supposedly mature heart *and* allow you to eat and drink things that other adults left behind in adolescence. Across Lancaster, Jarrow and elsewhere, Space Raiders and Tizer are an acceptable snack and that is to be celebrated.

In non-league football these scenes have their regular props, not least the club lotto table. I have seen trestle and wallpapering tables used, or upturned boxes and planks resting on stools. They are always improvised and in their own way ingenious. Today, two cheerful volunteers in fluorescent vests stood behind a knee-high pedestal cabinet on wheels of the type usually buried within an office desk. Its drawers had been removed so that the apparatus of raffle – ticket books, Bic biros, a plastic Lloyds Bank change bag stuffed plump with 50 pence pieces – could be stored in the cavity.

Operating their lotto beat with the disciplined efficiency of soldiers administering food parcels in a war zone, all that could foil these hi-vis heroes was the rising breeze. Impromptu weights – a tiny padlock from the metal float till, a set of car keys – were placed over ticket piles to stop the wind from carrying them off. Unfortunately, when one such item was needed, a hand whisked it away with little notion of the consequences. A gust of wind swelled and blew a twister of tickets high into the air and then swirled them around by the corner flag. The vested two grasped and grabbed to gather as many chits as they could muster. It looked like the final round of *The Crystal Maze*. As their table was on wheels, I spent much of the first half expecting to see it rattle towards the goal at the downhill end of the pitch, with those two chasing behind.

Beyond the main stand rested an open-ended mesh cage of eight feet high and four wide. At one end waited the now-empty pitch, at the other, the dressing rooms. A warm front of Ralgex floated its way towards those of us standing nearby. It seemed to headbutt fresh air out of the way. In those months when footballers were not allowed to play, the medicinal muscle relief industry must have entered a harsh recession. I began to wonder if those players might suffer withdrawal symptoms, so institutionalised within them have these scents become. I pictured them using

Deep Heat patches as smokers do with nicotine, or searching supermarkets for Vaseline air freshener.

As three o'clock chimed near, one by one the players strutted through the tunnel and on to the pitch. Observing them in this manner reminded me of watching the lunchtime penguin parade at a zoo, or wrestlers entering the arena. That latter feeling was enhanced by the swagger of Basford United right-back James Clifton. Shaven-headed but with a fulsome beard that could've provided comfortable lodgings for a family of ravens, Clifton possessed the steely glare of a fireman attending a cat rescue. Basford were managed by former Nottingham Forest centre-half Steve Chettle, a man who had seen that look many times before on the face of teammate Stuart Pearce. Perhaps he'd been coaching Clifton in the changing-room mirror.

With all players across the white line, the mesh tunnel was dragged backwards by two stewards, stagehands removing a prop. Those who had gathered could now move over this level crossing towards takeaway pints from Netbusters bar or their usual berths on the Shed End terrace behind the goal. The two teams were summoned to the centre circle for a minute's applause dedicated to care workers. Matchday ceased so that everyone could participate; in Dolly's Diner the tea stopped flowing and in the stands, veteran drinkers rested their plastic pint pots on walls. City wore an all-blue kit, United – or, the Lions – all-red. Lined up so rigidly now and in such generic colours, both resembled ultra-defensive table football teams. Upon the referee's whistle, they split as if ripped apart and thrown across the room by some livid schoolchild in a tantrum.

The whistle blew again and football had returned to Giant Axe. This was the first home league game of the season and through cheers and applause at kick-off, supporters in the Shed End made expressive eye contact with one another that seemed all at once to say 'Phew', 'It's good to be back' and 'I hope it lasts'.

In the time of Covid, each fan of each club across the land kept in mind a particular moment or encounter that would symbolise, for them, football being properly *back*. For some, it was being once more in a certain pre-match pub or eating a burger with waxy onions from a particular catering van. Others looked forward to seeing those souls they only encountered at football and thought of now and again through lockdown days, or of hearing a catch-phrase bellowed from the permanently underwhelmed bloke in the row behind – a 'Close him down, CLOSE HIM DOWN' or a 'Bloody useless, City, bloody useless'.

When the 15:03 Northern Rail train to Barrow skated along the West Coast main line above Giant Axe, I wondered if some Dolly Blues were living their 'We're back' moment. For them, I imagined, it would only truly be a homecoming when some spectators had their eyes robbed from the ball and kidnapped by a passing locomotive. To see a ground from a train is a delight, and so too is seeing a train from a ground. There are few greater theatres for this than Giant Axe. So close is Lancaster Station that, for a while, less well off – or simply more miserly – support-ers paid a tuppenny for a platform ticket and watched matches from there.

In truth, it would be hard for even the most optimistic home fan to believe that football here had settled comfortably back into its old rhythms. Every person in a terraced area stood upon a socially distanced cross, alone or in their friends and family 'Rule of Six' bubble. It was marked out by ticker tape in waspish black and yellow, stage marks for pandemic spectating.

Ticker tape was used, too, to denote which main stand seats could be used – it was draped tightly across forbidden chair backs in the manner of rope around a hostage's chest – and to designate separate routes to Dolly's Diner, Netbusters bar and the Gents toilets. In that area, it made for something of a chal-lenging maze. Later on, during the second half, I heard a man reach the front of the queue for Dolly's and tell the woman behind the counter: 'I only wanted a pee.' Lancashire had its Bermuda Triangle and it was made entirely of yellow and black ticker tape.

Further, from the public address system came a recorded Covid safety message in a tone so sombre that I swear I saw a tear trickle down the face of a passing pigeon, and stewards reminded any supporter moving around to wear a face mask. After the first such intervention, each time a steward passed by one bloke near me cried 'Bloody Gestapo' and 'Hey up, here's Stasi' in a Lancastrian accent so strong that it knocked over a nearby industrial chimney.

Most Shed dwellers, however, complied peacefully and looked on sanguinely. They sat on the terrace's broad steps or leaned against its toothpick beams. Teenagers chewed on Capri Sun straws, their version of Clint Eastwood's matchstick, and sang 'I'd rather be a Dolly than a Shrimp', a reference to local rivals Morecambe. In front of them, Lancaster's bald defensive duo Niall Cowperthwaite and Andrew Teague chased nimble Basford forward Rev James around like two mad bulls pursuing a mongoose. When any Dolly Blues player got close to James, they seemed afraid to make a challenge. Perhaps each of them presumed that the Basford man was a real, ordained reverend and fouling him would be akin to punching someone wearing glasses.

The Lions tried to shift the ball around quickly. They swarmed forward with the enthusiasm and carelessness of seven-year-old boys dive-bombing into a ball pool. 'Have they got more players than us?' said a man standing alone on his cross behind me. Therein lay another reason why being back at the match was a good thing: in very few other circumstances can you talk out loud to no one in particular and face no consequences for your actions. At football, people nod along or even reply, something unimaginable of the loner talking to himself outside a city centre branch of Argos.

Basford's plot of passing rapidly and invading in great numbers as if someone had shouted 'Last orders at the bar' was thwarted by the playing surface. The Giant Axe turf seemed somehow clumpier and denser than that of other grounds. It made for a gloopy species of football where passes seemed to plod rather than roll and long balls landed stock still with the thud of a bag of sugar falling on to sand. The grass was long and in one hallucinogenic moment later on, I became convinced that it was visibly growing during the match, so that by the end players would be submerged and only able to call for the ball by releasing distress flares.

Drifting towards the long terrace nearest the railway line, I encountered a disused scoreboard by the corner flag. Its rusty squares where nils and threes were once displayed now sat empty, 'Lancaster' and 'Visitors' forever drawing a blank. Thoughts of the ethereal and of the bygone footballers who once animated those spaces were punctured by incessant whistling from the referee. He had managed to irritate and aggravate the players of both teams in equal measure, an achievement of sorts. It was a shame to witness him being treated so angrily; with his fine grey moustache and abundant belly, he seemed like the kind of amiable chap who should've been spending his Saturday afternoons offering advice on creosote and sealant guns in a DIY superstore rather than shouting 'Get away, number 5' to men 40 years his junior.

With 25 minutes gone, he awarded Basford a corner in front of the ghost scoreboard. Matt Thornhill – a wily attacking midfielder once of Nottingham Forest and Hibernian – hoisted the kick so that it seemed to hang in the air like a Chinese lantern. Dolly Blues goalkeeper Sam Ashton pawed fruitlessly at the ball and Basford's Stef Galinski clonked a header goalwards. In the previous season, Galinski had scored with his head from Basford's own half. Now, his point-blank effort was being cleared from behind the line by a Lancastrian player who fell into the net and became hopelessly entangled. He resembled a spider in the wrong web. Perhaps dreaming of grout pens or cordless drills, the referee looked on motionless. His linesman flagged to indicate the ball had breached the goal line. One-nil to Basford, not that the scoreboard showed even a flicker. 'Fucking Nora,' shouted a home fan near me.

In the lull after the goal, a Basford fan struck up conversation with a local, both men on their marks. Draped in a yellow scarf and staring absent-mindedly at the pitch as if it were a vast and empty ocean and they were on the bow of a trawler, he began a gentle and reflective soliloquy on his supporting life. 'It's love, I suppose. I were born into it. No choice in the matter. Yellow and black blood. I could've followed the trophies at Forest, but you can't fake how you feel. I go to every game, home and away. Not that they notice.'

Over at the West Road End, continuing his impartial mission to aggrieve both sides equally, the referee handed Lancaster a free-kick in the corner junction where touchline meets penalty area. The ball was rolled five yards to Tom Kilifin and in attempting to whip in a snappy cross, he struck it with the wrong part of his foot. It moved in the unpredictable manner of a potato rolling across a kitchen floor, bobbing and cavorting its way towards goal. This trajectory bamboozled those in red, who flailed and seemed to perform a rain dance around it. A yard in front of an empty goal, centre-half Teague skewered the ball in to equalise. Fists clenched, he celebrated by howling loudly at the empty net, the dad who had finally won his daughter a giant Winnie the Pooh at the coconut shy. The home crowd cheered with the kind of fervour that must have awoken snoozing museum attendants in the castle above. It felt as though they were acclaiming more than just a goal and letting out noise that had dwelled dormant within them for months. Their right to make indecipherable yowls of elation had been restored.

In the minutes before the interval, dense clouds slithered apart and for the first time all day the sun blasted through. It turned the pitch and stands from soot to fairy dust. What had been murky now shone and being inside a football ground felt like an enormous slice of good fortune. The Basford monologist had now begun a passage on the club's history ('In 1904, we could've gone into the Football League instead of Chelsea'). His previously silent audience of one had lost the thread and possibly the will to live. When the goalscorer, Teague, clobbered a clearance towards a passing train, he broke his hush with a cry of 'Woah, Toblerone boots. You trying to send that ball to London?'

At half-time I negotiated the ticker tape labyrinth and joined the bar queue in Netbusters. The wait gave me time to ponder the club-shop price list, a piece of orange card inside a punched pocket folder. Items for sale were neatly handwritten in felt-tip – 6" Rulers 50p, Lancaster City Bookmark £2 and all the rest. The list and every other detail, hatch and crevice of Giant Axe spoke of devotion and volunteering and hours spent in the name of keeping Lancaster City breathing because, in the end, towns need football clubs.

By now, the bar was running low on supplies. 'Pint of bitter please, darling,' asked the man in front of me. 'We've no ale left. Only Guinness,' she replied. Horrified at such a thought, his reaction was somehow poetic: 'No thanks, cock. Guinness tastes of horse.'

I carried my pint to the West Road terrace and rested it on a crush barrier. On the pitch, a club volunteer with a backpack full of disinfectant sanitised the goalposts with all the relish of a man looking at somebody else's holiday photos. I looked around at the hotchpotch of stands, adapted cargo containers and signs painted and affixed in a hundred different fonts. It was a joyous thing to again be in one of these oddball, endlessly interesting and completely unique constructions. Grounds like this are organic and change just as a domestic house does – whenever it needs to, or when the money or materials are found to make alterations. They are loved in the same way as family homes, but by many thousands of people through several generations. 'All Dollies, Aren't We?' asked a flag hung from the terrace wall, and I began to think that there were many worse things to be.

Half-time contemplation over, I moved back to the Shed End in anticipation of Dolly Blue goals. A drove of teenage lads had gathered hoping for the same. Seizing on Lions goalkeeper Kieran Preston's ginger hair and alabaster skin, they began a round of 'Two Ed Sheerans/There's only two Ed Sheerans…' It was only when Preston turned to them with arms aloft that they realised Basford had scored a second goal.

This time, a thunderous tackle by Lancaster midfielder Paul Dawson catapulted against Teague's knees and landed at the feet of Rev James. He bumbled the ball into the six-yard box, where Alex Howes scored from a distance of 12 inches. Despite this proximity, Howes weltered his strike as if playing in the park and wishing to force a goalkeeping friend into fetching the ball from a distant field.

The Lancaster ultras responded with sustained ballads about Dollies and Shrimps. They bayed their team forward and heralded corners as if cheering backed horses at the finishing line. Meanwhile, slightly younger children clambered over one another to reach at coins in what seemed to be a 1920s penny scramble game. Under-14s paid no entrance fee at Giant Axe, and it transformed the ground into an extension of their gladdening places and playgrounds. It gave them somewhere to be, and a space for being young and daft. How they had been robbed of that in this poxed year.

They needed their songs and distractions to revel in, because Basford were now shredding through Lancaster with ease. The away side had adjusted to the feral playing surface just as eyes adapt to the dark. Conducting the orchestra was Kyle Dixon, a slight midfielder whose nifty passing seemed to lift his teammates. Rev James revealed a kind of hoax in which he moved as if in treacle to lull opponents forward and then skipped beyond them in a whirl. 'You're getting beat by a man in gloves, Lancaster,' cried a man to my left. 'GLOVES.' Left-back Ryan Wilson, his long mane flopping like a pancake being flipped, executed a drop-shouldered dummy of rare beauty and poise. He followed it up by spooling the ball over the stand as if to demonstrate that he was normal like everyone else.

With quarter of an hour remaining, the Dollies began to retaliate, hauling their way towards the Basford box in increments. They should have equalised when Teague ascended and met a clipped free-kick with a glancing header. He seemed to urge the ball towards the goal as if a delicate touch could coax it home like a hen lured into the coop. Preston leaped and toppled it wide. A few minutes later, Teague's defensive partner Cowperthwaite found himself on the penalty spot, alone with the ball and only the goalkeeper in front of him. He wore the panicked expression of a cartoon felon under a police helicopter's searchlight. Having found the wherewithal to swing back a leg and shoot, he missed the ball entirely and fell over.

Captain Teague spurred his side on and hurtled balls forward. One last effort, though, remained suspended in the air for so long that the weather seemed to change before it fell. Fat clouds once more swaddled the sun and everyone knew there would be no equaliser. The final whistle sounded and one Shed End man asked of another, 'What *has* gone wrong this season?' 'Bloody hell, Frank,' replied his friend, 'we've only played two games.'

With the mesh tunnel retracted, supporters and volunteers meandered homewards or stopped to moan their way through the result. This ritual of instant analysis, mutual therapy and brow-beaten grousing was something, deep down, they had missed as much as goal celebrations or matches by floodlight.

'See you Tuesday night, love,' said a man in a club blazer to a steward making her way towards the exit gate. 'Hope so,' she replied, now holding up two sets of crossed fingers. 'I really do.' It was a reminder that the fixtures we so cherished were written in pencil, not ink.

3

Workington 2 v 0 Mossley
Northern Premier League
Division One North West

It was Bill Shankly's first day in the job as Reds manager. He shoved a door, entered the darkness and ran his hand around the wall as if auditioning as a plasterer's apprentice. 'What you doing?' came a voice from the abyss. 'I'm putting on the light,' Shankly replied. There was no electric illumination, the boss learned. Only gas. Workington AFC in January 1954 was a gas lamp kind of club.

He walked on. His steel-capped brogues beat a tick-tock rhythm on the floor. It echoed among Borough Park's concrete walls as if a teaspoon regiment was invading. As usual, Billy Watson, Workington's devoted groundsman, was sitting in the boiler room. It was the only warm space in the ground, an oven amid igloos. He could hear the new manager getting closer. His feet were a countdown. The door swerved ajar. 'What's that awful smell?' growled an Ayrshire miner's voice. 'That's my cats,' said Watson. 'Either they go or I go,' fired back the miner. They stayed.

Shankly's eyes and nose had been offended and assaulted. Now it was time for his ears. Down the tunnel had drifted hollers and thuds. 'What's going on?' he asked now. 'That's the Rugby League,' he was told. 'What do you mean, the Rugby League?' When they sold Shankly the job, his new Reds board had neglected to mention the groundshare. This was Thursday evening. Thursday evening was Workington Town RLFC's training slot.

The Scotsman wore the look of a man arriving home from work to find that his mother-in-law had unexpectedly moved in. He strode towards the pitch, a one-man stampede. 'What the hell are you doing?' said the football manager to his rugby colleague. 'We're scrumming!' replied Gus Risman, the 41-year-old player-coach who had recently led Town to a momentous Challenge Cup win. Seventy-two thousand had been there at Wembley that day, 19 April 1952, the same afternoon that Shankly's Grimsby Town, of Division Three (North), played out a draw against York City at Bootham Crescent. 'Christ!' offered the soccer man. 'There's a football game on Saturday here.'

Shankly pleaded for the playing surface and in the dialect of the coalfields beseeched the scrummers to toddle off. Later, he quarrelled with Risman about pitch width, howling that the white lines of football were sacrosanct. Narrowing them was like redrawing a sacred chalk hill figure in crayon. He would make his case – the cause of the turf's sanctity – in rambunctious board meetings too. That board, though, was 'laced with rugby league directors', said Bill. Besides, Reds could not afford to evict their tenants.

Workington AFC were £20,000 in debt. The rent that their oval-ball lodgers supplied was vital, even if it bought them the right to pillage and scuff Shankly's pitch. In clement months it was a marsh; when winter came, a clotted ice rink. Every Saturday it groaned as players of both sports inflicted a million studded pockmarks, an acne outbreak in the sticky mud.

Sometimes, both teams trained or played on the same day. Watson remembered 80 people training at once and recalled a Reds fixture with Oldham Athletic. At 4.45pm, its 5,000 spectators left. At 5pm, 21,000 Town supporters filed in to watch their team. That attendance deficit spelled a truth: Workington was a town married to rugby. Now Shankly, that great missionary with a whistle around his neck, had to make it flirt with soccer.

It was, too, a small place of 25,000 people and a poor one of spent mines, waning shipyards and steelworks forever battling to stay conscious. Nessie, Bill's wife, called it 'bleak' and told how a veneer of grime would descend on washing left too long on the clothes line.

Workington is geographically exiled on England's left shoulder blade. On 1950s tarmacadam, it took two hours to reach local derbies with Barrow and Carlisle United. The club was elected to the Football League in 1951 and finished its first season in last place and its second a position above. Shankly's predecessor, Ted Smith, resigned so that he could go and work in a prison. At the beginning of the month in which Workington directors started to try and entice him from Grimsby, December 1953, the team was bottom of the league once more. In late October, they had lost 8-0 at Wrexham. Bequeathed such a barren context, the Scotsman needed allies. In Billy Watson, he found more than that: he won a dear friend, moggies and all.

The manager's office, a fusty wooden hut, reeked of damp and possessed the climate of a Siberian larder. It made sense to huddle in Watson's boiler room. When the groundsman heard clippety-clop shoes, he knew that the boss was on his way. Shankly would bring a lemonade crate to sit on. Kicking to one side half-used tins of paint with dry drips lapping, beneath the forks and spades of Watson's trade the two would talk.

Almost always, their conversation threw them backwards to halcyon Saturdays. The manager enthused on his playing career and the greats he'd encountered. The groundsman spoke of the games and wizards he had seen. There would be time for industrial reflections as well – the Scot on his mining days, the Cumbrian on his steelwork toils. When the great man moved on to conquer the world, they remained pen pals. At Shankly's funeral in 1981, Workington were represented by a tearful Billy Watson.

It helped their kinship that, somehow, by Shankly's second season in charge – 1954/55 – Watson had nurtured the Borough Park pitch into something of a marvel. 'You have to dedicate yourself to it,' he would go on to say. 'You haven't got to look at the clock. This is my way and where I'll always be.' In 1976, former

Workington defender Keith Burkinshaw became Tottenham Hotspur manager. He invited the Cumbrian to look after the White Hart Lane turf. Watson declined, later reflecting that 'I wouldn't have liked London… Workington are my life.'

Shankly had been persuaded to leave Grimsby by Reds directors – at a Blackpool hotel, no less – in the days leading up to Christmas 1953. There were two reasons for departing the Mariners, beyond his young daughters' complaints about the town smelling of fish: he had taken an ageing team as far as he could, and both he and Nessie were homesick for Ayrshire. It may have been marooned from most of England, but Workington to Scotland was not too much of a stretch.

Shankly's new club were tormented by the thought of returning to non-league just three years after absconding. Despite this, optimism reigned upon his arrival in January 1954. 'Shankly's born enthusiasm for anything he tackles', posited the *Lancashire Evening Post*, 'should soon create a new and more enthusiastic spirit in the Workington camp.' The man himself said: 'If I did not think I could pull Workington out of their trouble, I would never have left Grimsby. I am sure I shall be happy here.' That bullish spirit transmitted to the club's supporters. Thirteen thousand of them attended Shankly's first match in charge, drawn 2-2 in the Cumbrian derby with Carlisle United. A month later, a thousand more watched the 2-0 defeat of Port Vale, runaway leaders and eventual Division Three (North) champions. 'Reds Greatness Has Been the Talk of the Town' read a headline in the local paper. The flirtation was well and truly under way.

Fans' optimism and enthusiasm proved to be well founded. Workington heaved themselves up the division and secured survival before the season's end. Beneath the headline plaudits and happy chants came explanations for Shankly's success that would be heard time and again over the following decades. His team had a formidable togetherness, laboured for one another and adhered to the Scotsman's commandments, disciplinary and otherwise. Stories of an ilk now familiar emerged: on Friday nights in away game hotel lounges, at 10.30pm precisely, Shankly would glance dramatically at his watch. Players were expected to immediately rise and then retire to bed. He guarded the foyer just in case of daring – or foolish – jailbreakers.

It helped that the Scotsman was visible in town and omnipotent at Borough Park. Each weekday morning, he would walk the mile there from the family home on Harrington Road. Come midday, he would return for lunch with Nessie, and then repeat the route. There were tasks to perform beyond the contested turf or the tactics board.

Workington, said Shankly, 'was a shoestring club'. Staff were thin on the ground. His graft would have to suffice. Telephone Borough Park on any day between early 1954 and late 1955 and you may well have been greeted by a gruff Ayrshire voice. Receptionist Shankly also opened the mail, replying to every missive with a phone call or typewritten letter. He became the recognised face of Reds, a walking club badge, accepting invitations to events and openings, whether judging beauty contests or participating in charity games. One July afternoon in 1954, he refereed a game at Borough Park between Dick, Kerr Ladies and a visiting Parisian side.

Every Thursday, it was Shankly's job to collect the squad's wage packets from the bank, wedge them into his pockets and then waddle through town and back to the ground. He was convinced he would be mugged, but the only money he ever parted with on those errands was his own – without fail, he would stop to talk to gangs of unemployed steelworkers who loitered on street corners and then hand them a couple of shillings each. The Scotsman even donated a fine suit to one of them, 'Old Foster'. Sewn into its inside pocket was the name 'Bill Shankly'. Not that Foster would ever forget it.

This furrowed and dogged town was Shankly's kind of place. In the autumn of 1954, he spoke of his trust in 'the North' – which seems, for him, to have encompassed an industrial belt coiling from the Tyne to the Clyde – and its footballers. His musings seem ideological, as if he were theorising in search of a formula for success on a grand scale. 'I'll get into trouble for saying this,' he told the *Daily Mirror*, 'but my theory is that real players are born and the exceptions among the Southerners are merely throw-backs to a Northern Ancestry. It is my firm conviction that the better football is played in the North. If I had an assignment – and an open chequebook – to build myself a brand-new side, in two or three seasons they would be world beaters. And I wouldn't move a yard south from Carlisle.'

That summer, in the pre-season prior to his first full term as manager, Shankly had put another of his theories into practice. His success in enticing the board into paying all its players the same wage was evidence of the ex-miner's unfussy socialism. It was testament to the might of his persuasive powers too – he had negotiated a raise to £14 per week, the division's highest. Penny-pinching was for other parts of the club; those well-remunerated players trained beneath the beams of lights powered by an old bus engine, and used brown balls painted white to satisfy new league regulations. Not that such deprivations would be tolerated as excuses. 'Every player is under an obligation to give good enter-tainment to the public,' he told the *Workington Star* in August. 'May I stress that we will do our best to see that the crowd's loyalty is well and truly rewarded.'

Nourished by fine team spirit and a variety of incisive, hare-footed football, by Christmas Workington were firm title contenders. The *Star* labelled their playing style 'a shimmering Shankly pattern'. The manager even chiselled advantage from his club's geographic alienation. In team talks he would claim that he had watched opponents arriving at Borough Park appearing squeamish. 'They look sick,' he would say. 'It's that road from Keswick. They're finished. No trouble today, boys.' It was all part of the Shankly ploy to make his men feel indestructible and to refuse defeat as if it were a simple yes or no question. In training matches, full-time only came when his team was in the lead. It was a practical demonstration that successful sides needed to be stubborn and bend fate with their bare hands. Where there was a will there was a way. His way.

Though forever bickering – Shankly said attending a board meeting was 'as good as going to the music hall' – the club's directors launched a 'Prepare for Promotion' plan that pledged a raft of future investment. There was a fine FA Cup victory at Leyton Orient, too. The day before, Shankly had learned that his great heroes, the Hungary team, were in a first-class carriage of the *Flying Scotsman* train he and his squad boarded at Carlisle. The Mighty Magyars had that week defeated Scotland 4-2 at Hampden Park, and Shankly walked his players from second class to see them, a dozen children and their dad scrambling to meet a team of Santa Clauses. The two squads talked of similarities and differences between being the greatest in the world and Division Three (North). Shankly used coins, matches and anything else close by to demonstrate set-piece routines to Puskás, Hidegkuti, Kocsis and friends. That Friday evening, his players went to watch *Cinderella on Ice* in the West End.

This weekend of untold glamour proved to be the season's zenith. Workington faded away and finished eighth. It was still a fine accomplishment for a club previously unacquainted with the division's higher reaches. Shankly was moulding footballers and coaxing them into performing beyond their individual potential as part of a resilient, vibrant unit. It was as if he was writing in pencil the pages of a future manifesto for supremacy.

Amid that backdrop, and in a town increasingly aware it was standing on the shoulders of an infant giant, season 1955/56 began with promotion hopes high and rising. By early winter, those hopes looked like being realised. Workington were title contenders again. In October, 13,029 saw their team pulverise Carlisle United 4-0. Yet that rosy crowd masked a malaise. It was a blip. Gates of five or six thousand and dwindling were more common. The board continued to barney its way through. Money grew scarcer. The players accepted a wage cut and Shankly did the same in solidarity, a despondent kind of socialism.

Victories were still notched, but Bill knew, organs deep, he had done everything he could. Too much of the town had returned to its stable marriage with rugby. Workington would never sate his ambitions. Andy Beattie, an old teammate from Preston North End and Scotland and now Huddersfield Town manager, called. The offer of an assistant manager post was made. Bill deliberated – this place, these lads, were under his skin, and what of Billy Watson? – but aspiration overcame stagnant loyalty. He was gone by Christmas. 'He was a god in Workington,' said forward Jack Bertolini, scorer of the winner at Brisbane Road and in the summer months a borer with the Coal Board. 'When he left, it dropped off, an era had passed.' Watson reflected that 'He did the right thing. I didn't want him to go but he had to go on to somewhere better.'

Twenty-five years after the manager left for West Yorkshire, he and Watson cut the ribbon on a new bar within the Borough Park main stand, The Shankly Lounge. Shankly called it the greatest honour of his career, beyond, even, any Anfield-won trophy. 'I put it above that because I was only here for a short space of time and people remember me for it. That's something great. Football is a hard-bitten game and sometimes people forget what a man has done, but Workington didn't forget, and I've done more for other teams than I did for Workington. It is a very rich honour.'

* * *

'Hello, Workington 602871,' said the genial old man answering the Borough Park telephone. It was an instant and pleasant repatriation to an era Shankly would have recognised. I could not recall the last time I'd been greeted with town-then-number; it died out with grandmas who resembled Aunt Bessie and then landlines themselves.

With the ground's attendance capacity curtailed by Covid regulations, it seemed prudent to call in advance and reserve a ticket, and now here I was, talking like it was 1992. Even as we spoke, I felt like hanging up and trying some of the landline numbers of my youth, as if a friend's dad might once again pick up instead of being lost to time or some horrible disease. In another comforting sign that not all the old ways were gone, no payment would be taken for my ticket until later, when 'someone who understands all that stuff' was to call me back. Inside the unseeing world of the phone call, I imagined Shankly and Watson in their boiler room, dealing cards and waiting for the old man to rejoin them.

I had arrived in Workington under a sky shaded in the lethargic grey of an old 50 pence piece. Illumination came from the railway station's vintage maroon and cream signage, the verbena and salvia of its cheerful flower beds and the lurid livery of a boy racer's Subaru. The car's exhaust backfired, making the noise of a stifled musket at a historical re-enactment, and an old woman raised and waggled her walking crook in admonishment, like a furious shepherd.

Inside a glass display window on the station wall, an A4 sheet entitled 'Autumn and Winter Day Trip Programme 2020' offered excursions to Bury Market, Blackpool Illuminations and elsewhere. A number of outings had been struck through in black marker pen; there would be no Beamish and Metro Centre, and no Edinburgh Xmas Markets now. This was, after all, the era of cancellations, postponements and 'Hopefully next year's. Lines of redaction had been drawn across the name of every place on the map and every notch on the clock.

On the walk towards Workington town centre, more signs spoke of moments in time: first, elevated on the gable end of an old building, a faded advertisement for The Oxford, a 'temperance hotel' with 'luncheons and teas' on offer; then, in a small civic garden, a European-Union-blue road sign pointing the way to 'Selm, Germany, 1005km', this Cumbrian town's twin. A quarter of its surface was taken up by the 12 yellow stars of the EU standard, erected in a period of local enthusiasm for the European project. In the 2016 referendum, 60 per cent of locals had voted Leave.

Around the corner, a plaque fastened to a red-brick hangar proclaimed March 19th 1926, when it became 'The first purpose-built covered bus shelter in Great Britain'. This seemed to me a worthy event to mark – one of those small advancements in a place that for a while is the talk of the town, and when it arrives improves the lives of locals in some slight, and yet meaningful, way.

Their modern equivalents filed by and slipped down busy and narrow pedestrianised streets. From the hatch of a truck, Wayne of Wayne's Market Meats peddled his carcasses and offcuts beneath a red-and-white stripy awning. There were beef roasts for £10 each and four salmon steaks for a fiver, all of it 'Fresh & Safe to Freeze' according to one of Wayne's many chalkboards. A man and a woman paused to hear today's specials and then began speaking.

'You out tonight, John?'

'Dunno. Out Monday an' all, aren't I? *She'll* not be happy.'

'But it's Tanya's leaving do.'

'Well, exactly.'

'Oh yeah.'

It was a comment left to hang in the air until the two's dialogue was shut down by half a dozen teenage lads on BMXs racing by in front of them. 'Christ's sake,' offered John, 'it's getting like E bleedin' T round here.'

More plaques were freckled around town, most of them dedicated to Rugby League heroes such as Eppie Gibson and Billy Ivison. Ivison, in fact, had a whole street named after him, as did Bill Shankly's tenant, Gus Risman. The oval's triumph over the spherical proved long-standing in Workington.

At the end of Risman Place, a pleasant sculpture installation named *Coastline* boasted rock 'sentinels' that 'double as bins', perhaps giving them an air of mystery when they attended parties. Across from *Coastline*, the discreetly noble Theatre Royal's doors remained bolted. There would be no treading the boards and no mums writing 'Pantomime' on the family planner anytime soon ('Hopefully next year…'). Even in present football's reduced and furtive guise, having our own floodlit playhouses to attend felt suddenly a privilege.

Public art besides *Coastline* could be found across the town centre, pockets of cheer, storytelling and intrigue in a tough old place. A giant mechanical steel clock and musical benches channelled elements of Willy Wonka's factory. Such pieces seemed all the more surreal when sighted outside Shoe Zone and JD Sports. Down an alley between two chain stores was *Sailgates*, a craggy iron barrier inadvertently resembling crumpling police riot shields in line. Installed to recognise Workington's former shipbuilding prowess, it is inspired by the story of *Ada Iredale*, a locally constructed barque. In 1876, her cargo of a thousand tons of coal had caught fire. The *Iredale* crew abandoned ship in the South Pacific, and she drifted for eight months until being stopped by a French cruiser, fire still raging, and towed to Tahiti. It is a story that feels like a metaphor or allegory I can't quite fathom.

I took a seat on Curwen Place. It was named after John Christian Curwen, a reforming local MP. In the 1820s, he had attempted to highlight rural poverty by attending Parliament dressed as a local labourer, and carrying a block of cheese and a loaf of bread under each arm. Now, his square hosted a lone pillar made from steel donated by the local Moss Bay plant before it closed in 2006. Its output of rail way tracks cover the world; the factory's loss and accompanying industrial decline savaged Workington. For a good while, there have been plenty of unemployed men on corners that Shankly could've talked to.

More BMX bikers settled on the next bench and alternated between wheelies and idle chatter. When a man in his thirties walked by, they stopped him and enquired where he'd bought his trainers from. His reply of 'London' was met with mocking coos. 'Posh bastard,' said one of the teenagers, which solicited a wink and a thumbs up from trainers man. 'Cheers,' he said, before swaggering off.

I walked by the Miners Arms, a pub Shankly would have passed on his daily strolls from Harrington Road to Borough Park and back. Perhaps he thought fleetingly of the Ayrshire pits and the altogether different life he'd known underground. Close by, Nook Street led to pretty if careworn lanes, and soon the breeze ushered towards me the tannoy psalms and sermons of matchday.

* * *

A fortnight had passed since my visit to Lancaster. Football had survived and lower-level matches could still permit spectators. The crossed fingers of that Dolly Blues steward had come good.

Speckles of optimism could occasionally be felt. HOPES GROW FOR VACCINE, *The Times* had pronounced the previous Saturday. That afternoon I'd attended Carlisle City versus Birtley Town in rain that fell with the persistence of a child begging for a toy during the festive season. At half-time, three men with brooms had tried to sweep water from the pitch but succeeded only in creating a minor lagoon in front of the Sizzle burger van. Interminable raindrops made a soothing, pacifying sound as they landed on the aluminium roof of the stand. From underneath, it alternated between sounding like popcorn in a microwave and the frizzy noise in between stations on pre-digital radios.

Afterwards, in the Gents toilets of the Railway Social Club next door, I saw a man attempting to dehydrate the stomach of his jumper in the warm air of an automatic hand dryer. Unfortunately, what he took to be that dryer was in fact a paper towel dispenser. He looked me in the eye through the mirrors above the sinks. 'Well, this is bloody broken,' he said, before stomping off to complain. It was that kind of day.

Followers of clubs in higher divisions saw those crowds gathered in Cumbria and elsewhere and pondered why they remained banished from the terraces, filthy rainfall or not. A public petition to Parliament under the banner 'Let The Fans Back In' quickly gathered 200,000 signatories. Yet this never felt like a campaign gaining momentum towards some glorious return, more a defiant protest march before an air force dropped its bombs anyway. The only thing gaining momentum was the gathering folklore that, soon, Covid restrictions would once more tighten, again closing even the modest stadiums of Jarrow, Lancaster, Workington and all the rest.

Today, though, splendid Borough Park could not hear the tittle-tattle, and the canvas before me looked exactly as it should. Crooked-backed men in flat caps tramped towards the ground while kids wearing scarves that dangled below their knees scrambled to keep pace. From a hundred metres across the road, its crimson walls stood out cheerfully against the grumpy sky. It was like spotting a friend in a room of strangers.

Closer inspection turned the painting into a joyous animation of what a football ground should look like. Corrugated fences and gates in dazzling red, battered handsome by age and clutching stories within, lined the walls. Some wore old signs carrying gate numbers for capacity crowd control unneeded and unheeded since the Shankly heyday. Mossy roofs protected The Tony Hopper Bar and the club offices, now fully electric. Stewards gathered outside, a mustering of fluorescence and fingerless gloves. 'How's me tea?' said one, repeating a question posed of him by a colleague. ''Ot and wet and nowt else matters.'

The ground's wooden main stand had, understandably, been pulled down in the wake of the 1985 Valley Parade disaster, and yet hints of it remained. The layers of an old home such as this one make for an animate kind of archaeology, as if time is no longer linear and the past breathes the same air as the present. Look long enough at a few remaining threadbare steps and you may become convinced that the snake's hiss of a wooden rattle can be heard.

A 'Sold Out' information plate had been bolted on to the specimen fixture board – sponsored by Sandwith Roofing, 'Supporting the Reds in their next home game' – to the upset of two Mossley fans. At the office door, they chanced and pleaded in quarry-deep west Pennine voices. 'Surely you can squeeze two more in, lad. We won't go near any other bugger. And we won't say owt if you don't.' 'Sorry lads, the rules are the rules. It's this bloody lurgy in't it.' I told them about the old steps I'd found – a closed-off portal that had once led to the motorway that runs above the ground. From there, most of the pitch could be seen. They looked blankly in my direction and mumbled something about a pub.

I made my way around the corner to a turnstile block, walking alongside the corrugated exterior of the south-west terrace. Its scarlet walls were sheltered by a roof that seemed to wear 50 years of weather all at the same time, like the face of an old fisherman. Red letters in a banner strapped to a fence pleaded that someone or other GIVE BOROUGH PARK A NEW LEASE OF LIFE. Earlier, I'd read in the *Workington Times and Star* about plans to flatten this ground and the neighbouring – and similarly characterful – home of the rugby club, Derwent Park. The two teams would share a bland new stadium in a Sports Village. Twenty-first-century Shanklys and Rismans could now anticipate a future generation of turf wars. Followers of both codes would watch their teams in generic surroundings. The age of the chain stadium was about to reach Workington. I sighed and let the turnstile's clanking groan take me to a splendid place that soon enough would be no more.

Inside, an old lady perched on a wooden stool, broadcasting a kind smile to all who entered. 'Programme, lad?' she asked me. 'That'll be £2.50, love.' She was simultaneously listening sympathetically to the troubles of a middle-aged man. It was a reminder that when football went missing, so did these encounters. A release valve was blocked, a particular problem among those who lived alone, for whom going to the match was a rare social, and sociable, occasion. 'Well, I'm sure you'll be OK, flower,' she told him.

The portal that reveals terraces, stands and the acid green of a pitch is always a saintly thing; that ascension inside never tires and always gratifies. To enter straight into the back of a terrace, as was the case here, though, is a rarefied version often lost to modern stadiums with their concourses and internal steps. It gives the feeling of going out on stage, the set and auditorium suddenly before you and fizzing.

Entering the scene before me were three generations of a family – grandma, her son, his son. She paused and turned slowly to her left, then fixed on a particular area of empty terrace over by the corner flag. I wondered if she was thinking of times and people that are no more. A football ground radiates with feelings like this – all of us can see ghosts. She stirred and came back around to the present. 'Ask your dad if he got his programme,' she called to her grandson, and he sprinted off on his search, a carrier pigeon begging questions about matchday rituals.

Three sides of Borough Park are, with the addition of a few seats, as they have long been: a staple-shaped continuous run of terracing. There are interlaced beams and sentry pillars that support roofs before giving way to open-air vantage points. Crush barriers in Forth Rail Bridge red puncture the ash-coloured concrete, art among the industry. Were Shankly to haunt this place, he would recognise it well. Ditto Matt Busby – his Babes played here in an FA Cup third-round tie in 1958, one month before the Munich air crash. I stood for a while and realised that I was in a living museum. Here was a football ground as football grounds used to be. It was like finding some vanished society alive and well.

From the uncovered north terrace, I watched the last minutes of Mossley's regimented warm-up routine. Players clipped first-time passes to each other. Their touches occasionally matched the drumbeats of the Motown records being spat from the tannoy system. I hoped that this was intentional – a piece of performance art football from the Harlem Globetrotters of Greater Manchester, perhaps. Then one of them hammered a ball with such surprising ferocity that it cleared the back of the terrace and bounced in the disused gravel area beyond. 'Fuck. That.' shouted the player. A coach dismissed him to collect the ball. 'Fifty quid, them are, son.'

The pitch cleared and just before 3 o'clock the 'Theme From Z-Cars' struck up. 'You've stolen Everton's music!' cried a visiting fan. As decreed by Covid-era rules, the teams took to the pitch separately, appearing as if they'd already had a row. Workington wore yet another shade of red, this time close to the maroon of a Gideon Bible. Their opponents – nicknamed the Lilywhites – sported white shirts with a black sash, and black shorts and socks, or 'stockings' as they must surely be called in a ground of Borough Park's vintage. Since their formation in 1903, the Lilywhites had been Cheshire and then Northern Premier League residents who seldom hinted at climbing any higher and were only rarely troubled by relegation. If they had a club motto, it might have been 'We're fine as we are, thanks'.

Workington, meanwhile, ceased being a Football League club in 1977 after several seasons of desperate fayre. Bill Shankly had been unemployed since 1974 – perhaps a call should've been made. Their league place was taken by Wimbledon. Since then, they had jolted between different levels of non-league and regional football, with money usually just as scarce as it had been in Shankly's day. 'We're out on a limb,' said a fan to me later that day. 'No sugar daddies, no highly paid players and no cash. Just a little club, but when you support Workington, you love them. You have to.'

Shortly after kick-off, the cloudy sky cracked wide open and the sun turned the pitch from army green to neon. I stood at the back of the terrace looking down to a game sprouting into life and then all across this vivid habitat. It gave a feeling of sanctuary and of being in exactly the right place at the right time. 'Come on Mossley/Come on Mossley' shouted a dozen or so Lilywhites, gladdened to be lost again in their tribal singsong.

A darting maroon figure pulled my roving eye back to the game. The charging man was young Reds left-back Liam Brockbank. He seemed to gallivant his way down the line, foxtrotting between flailing Lilywhite legs. Brockbank cultivated himself into a perfect crossing position. Opposing defender Sam Kilner thwacked the life out of him, a gin trap seizing a sprightly hare. The Mossley fans jeered and broke into their own version of *Que Será, Será*: 'Will I be Ashton? /Will I be Hyde? /Here's what she said to me...'

The subsequent free-kick was frittered but Workington continued to charge their way forward. Striker Ruben Jerome made a
habit of standing completely still and then dashing forward in
the manner of a man who had suddenly realised he was at the
wrong bus stop. Much of their play was inspired by midfielder
Brad Carroll, who had the affable and organised demeanour of a
top-rate best man on a stag do. He frequently snapped free from
those attempting to snuffle him in the centre of the pitch – among
them Mossley's Ethan Kershaw, whose ponytail swayed like a
flicked abacus all afternoon – and made scoring opportunities. 'I
don't like him being that far up, not one little bit,' said a Reds fan
near me. It brought to mind the kind of dad who uses the phrase
'Right, that's enough fun for one day'.

After a while, this snappy, biting start simmered. An unhur-
ried character to proceedings developed. It seemed to suit the pale
autumn light – this was kicking rusty leaves weather, not a time
of year for berserk exertion. The referee, a man in his sixties with
the mournful expression of a detective inspector briefing the media
outside court, aided this collective slouch. Each lecture he doled out
to players who had committed an offence became longer than the
last, to the extent that I began to wonder if he was delivering *actual*
lectures to them. Saturday afternoon at Borough Park was many
things, but possibly not the time and place for a bite-size recap on
Marx's *Theses on Feuerbach* or medieval Albanian tapestry.

Brockbank toiled to enliven play, the only awake toddler at
nursery naptime. He jigged around Kilner and spun in a cross. No
one was there. Jerome must have been waiting for some other bus.
The left-back jogged away wearing the irritated look of someone
who had returned to their mobile phone after an hour of charging
only to find they'd not switched the charger on at the socket.

Soon afterwards, Workington moved ahead with a suitably
lethargic goal. Brad Hubbold lofted a work-shy free-kick into
the box, the ball ricocheted around at a carpet bowls rather than
pinball pace, and forward Scott Allison dabbed the ball into the
net. Down in front of me, a bobble-hatted family raised their arms

in celebratory unison. Those days of Stay Home, Protect the NHS, Save Lives slogans seemed momentarily far removed, as if all of that had happened on another planet entirely. Goals are there to make us forget.

A number of Mossley players protested that Allison had been offside. This invited only a keynote speech from the referee – Industrial archaeology 1972 to 1985? The socialisation of technology in Canadian agriculture? – which was so lengthy that both sets of players might as well have sat on the grass like schoolchildren being read to beneath an oak tree. The contemplative mood was spiked a few minutes later when Workington's Louis Potts delivered a substandard corner and a teammate substitute warming up by the flag called out, 'Shite ball that, Louis'.

For the rest of the half, Workington drudged onwards. They were industrially relentless, a gradual yet willing traction engine of a team. For the Lilywhites, Kane Hickman – a gristly but able midfielder with the crew cut, lowered head and hunched shoulders of an AWOL soldier – chased down and pursued loose leads admirably, but this game was hard to rouse. Often, the home side would win a free-kick, then a corner from that set-piece, and subsequently fritter the corner. It was like reading a story in which every paragraph began with the same words.

At half-time I joined the queue in what had been The Shankly Lounge, now renamed The Tony Hopper Bar. Midfielder Hopper was a Reds great, playing 269 times for the club and captaining the side on 54 occasions. He had competed in a century of games for Carlisle United, and played for a time in Ireland too. In 2018, he died from motor neurone disease, aged just 42. Each of the bar signs inside and out featured his name above an illustration of a number 8 top. Behind the bar hung one of Hopper's shirts in a frame. 'Never Forgotten – Always a Red' read the words underneath.

Back outside, pre-match Motown had given way to mid-match D:Ream and then Gina G. It was a substitution that made me want to sing 'You don't know what you're doing' in the vague direction of the press box. A steward tripped over a step and a more senior steward with a clipboard came to his aid. He looked peeved to be filling in a health and safety form for a colleague, the wearied tradesman fixing a hole in his own roof.

There was more steward drama as I retook my place behind the goal for the second half. A couple of boys had scaled the back wall and were messing around in the scruffy area behind the stand. 'You two!' snapped the steward. 'Come back over 'ere. If I see you behind there again, yer out.' Softening, he added in a more concerned voice, 'It's dangerous, for one thing.' The lads looked scolded and yet amused, and it was easy to imagine they'd be doing impressions of the incident all evening and into next year. I found it, oddly, a comforting scene – the gruff-voiced 'Mister' telling off two mischievous kids as in a Janet and Allan Ahlberg book. The only thing missing was the threat of a clipped ear.

Early in the second half, with an opponent hustling him from behind, Workington right-back Jay Kelly rolled the ball under his foot several times. It was almost a kneading manoeuvre – the chef priming his delicate pastry. Then, faster than a blink, he twirled with the ball around his marker and ran to liberty. It was another moment of unexpected brilliance that left me pondering the fine margins between footballers of different levels. If a player could tease the ball to his will in that manner, why was he toiling in the eighth tier? Was the difference that great players could do such things nine or 10 times a match, and not just once? 'Oh fuck off!' shouted a Mossley fan as Kelly dashed away.

Throughout the rest of the game, Dan Wordsworth, a home centre-half, provided similar moments of distinguished skill, albeit more understated. Time and again, he anticipated a Lilywhite pass before its executer had even thought it up. Then, he would stride forward, always looking ahead for options that might shake his team into action. If overall the game was often an exercise in treading water, there was joy enough to be found in individual moments such as those that Kelly, Wordsworth,

Brockbank and others provided. Witnessing such skilful deeds is something to cherish wherever you watch football.

By contrast, Mossley's centre-forwards played with the polite unease of two men forced to go out for a pint by their more sociable partners. They seemed to be sharing the same pitch only because they had to. A tubby away supporter spluttered abuse at his team and then turned on Workington goalkeeper Jim Atkinson. 'Useless, you are,' he announced. 'Well, you paid to watch me!' replied Atkinson. The Mossley fan caused increasing irritation as the game proceeded. When he stumbled and almost fell over the hoarding and on to the pitch, followers of both clubs cheered. All humans need such a figure to unite them.

The sun lowered and Workington pushed onwards, albeit with the vigour of a yawning milkman at the end of his round. Winger Jordan Holt spun in a shot that curved majestically. It made Lilywhites keeper Liam Lovell back-pedal furiously, as if he were attempting to prevent a frisbee from landing on a barbecue, and tip the ball over. That interaction led to one of British football's great crowd noises: the collective 'Oooooh' for which mouths are shaped like Polo holes. It hung in the crisp autumn air, some cavernous birdsong.

With a few minutes remaining, Reds substitute David Symington slapped a free-kick towards goal from 30 yards out. It skimmed through the air, a leather drone, and bounced once before arriving in the far corner of the net. The crowd bellowed the satisfied, sated cheers of a guaranteed victory.

The light retreated further and the referee blew his final whistle. Arms previously acting as sun visors were raised aloft in applause. Hundreds looked to the same maroon 11 and grinned as they returned the claps. For what would not be the only time this season, 'Sweet Caroline' choked its way through the air. Borough Park felt like a cocoon set apart from the uneasy outside world.

Drifting out towards cars with heaters and results on the radio, or into town for a few celebratory pints, there was a familiar satisfaction about the way supporters talked and walked. All victories are shared. In the supermarket that separates the football and rugby grounds, a lady behind the cigarette counter asked a man in a red-and-white scarf what the score had been. 'Two-nil. Played well,' he replied. 'Aw, well done, love,' she responded, as if it were his victory. And it was.

Neither of them knew that this would be the last Saturday of football at Borough Park for nine months.

4

Kendal Town 0 v 3 Tadcaster Albion
Northern Premier League
Division One North West

Asphalt clouds loomed low over the fells, great ominous barrage balloons. They squashed the light out of everything and threatened to subsume the farmhouses that cling to Lake District peaks like fridge magnets. It was Halloween and the sky had come dressed as the grim reaper.

These conditions were in grumbling harmony with the national mood. England talked about the threat of a second lockdown even more than it talked about the weather or the past. Behind everyone hovered the same macabre shadow. Next time, when it came, there would be no novelty and no persistent sunshine, just isolation and rain. That evening, ghoulish costumes were not truthfully required – our faces were haunted masks.

Still, though, Westmorland's elegance was unperturbed. The steep peaks of Tarn Crag and its sister mountains gave way to smooth crests, a giant recreation of a hospital heart monitor suddenly flatlining. Torrents had lately nourished them into finer green shades than usual, and made their becks and streams froth and gurgle like jolly cauldrons. Impassive sheep clung on, unwittingly stoic.

Football was attempting to cling on too through this time of vulnerability and through the downpours. There grew from the game's spirit of perseverance a homespun form of innovation – bereft of fans, more and more clubs developed online streams so that games could be watched from home and a portion of lost revenues recouped. Some such systems worked better than others; some inadvertently provided laughter in a time when it was needed most. That very week, at Inverness Caledonian Thistle's Caledonian Stadium, a company named Pixellot had employed remote technology for the Scottish Championship fixture between the home side and Ayr United. Pixellot's AI camera was set to follow the ball, thus keeping up with play and beaming images of the game into thousands of homes. Unfortunately, it mistook bald linesman John McCrossan's head for that ball and for a while followed him instead. Viewers were left with footage of the lone McCrossan parading up and down his touchline. Ayr fans missed the build-up to their team's only goal in a 1-1 draw.

As I walked downhill from Oxenholme Station into Kendal, rainwater snuggled tightly to the kerb and formed a rapid gully guiding the way towards town. In the pleasant suburban homes that lined the way, net curtains parted and residents tutted and shook their heads at the sky. Over on the opposite side of the road, a man walked uphill with bare legs beneath a camel trench coat in the manner of a flasher from *Monty Python's Flying Circus*. As I averted my gaze and looked ahead again, a lady bearing several bloody scars offered cheerful greetings. The appearance of one of the pair could be explained away by Halloween. The other I will never, thankfully, know.

On the corner of Lound Road, a small sign pointed the direction to Kendal Town FC's Parkside Road ground. Taking that turn and spluttering its way by gracious Victorian limestone homes was the team coach of the Mintcakes' opponents that afternoon, Tadcaster Albion, nicknamed the Brewers. Seeing those words on a placard in the windscreen flew me a quarter of a century backwards to the middle years of my teens. Taddy were the finest team I played for across that decade-long sweet spot where nothing and no one else matters more than football.

Every now and then I look at our squad photo and I wonder what happened to them all. Pittsy, a centre-half who always wore his collar up and jumped into slide tackles as if impersonating a runaway bobsleigh. Grunt, then my best mate and a lad who simply could not be knocked off the ball – opponents who tried resembled moths ricocheting off a lightbulb. Browny, a sublime centre-midfielder and the only kid in school with adidas Predator boots. Beardmore, one of those boys so good that his name was known to other kids in other schools and of whom it was always said Leeds United scouts were watching. Cattle, our goalkeeper, a chubby yet dexterous lad whose long-haul clearances from back passes frequently bothered livestock in neighbouring fields. Hunty, a calm number 6 who once did a Cruyff turn on his own goal line…

Missing from the picture are the volunteers who gave their time so that we could play, just as they do across the land – men like our joint managers, the two Daves, and Pittsy's father, Big Trev. Big Trev was charged with treating our injuries, though his magic sponge – which looked suspiciously like a car shammy and even bore oil stains – never got near any player; a gruff shout of 'stamp it out' or 'run it off' was usually enough to scare any sprain or knock out of us.

Each of us in the photograph is 14 or 15. We look like thin impressionistic sketches of the men we will become. Our smiles are reserved but tangible, teenage embarrassment fused with an undercurrent of giddy glee – we were good, and boy did we know it. In the season the photo was taken, we won 19 of 20 league matches, drawing the other. The back four I was part of conceded 13 goals; 111 were scored, 53 of them by Grunt. We won the Main Cup and the League Cup, the Intermediate Minor Cup and others I became too blasé to even write down. Sunday mornings were the pinnacle of all our weeks. On Sunday afternoons, after another 8-0 or 12-1, without fail my grandma would pass me a pre-Sunday roast dinner glass of limeade and ask: 'Who were you playing? Blind School?'

Just before I put the photo down, I like to imagine what happened next. I can see us all moving away, sniggering, geeing one another along, welting Mitre Tactic balls, looking to the sidelines to see if a group of girls from school has shown up. I could lie and say that we were all full of hopes and dreams – ambitions that would see us into manhood. Our only dreams, however, were of being footballers, our only hopes that our dads would buy us chips after the game. I never again had a bunch of friends like those teammates I had when I was 14 years old. Bloody hell, who does?

Down in Kendal town centre, I sat and admired the poise and style of this antique place. However, even the certainty of its grand old buildings and the intrigue of its narrow alleyways could not offer sufficient reassurance or distraction; an invisible mist of collective worry induced sighs and prompted anxious conversations. Three old ladies gathered near me, their exchange summarising this malaise and its bleak humour. 'Everyone's saying lockdown's coming back,' started one. 'Oh I hope not. I'll not cope,' replied her friend. 'I hate lockdown, me,' offered the third. 'We're getting locked down at 4pm, I've heard,' continued the first. 'Oh heck. I'd better get my hair fluffed,' said the second.

In WH Smith's, this melancholy tension seemed to permeate through a pensioner's exasperation at a young shopworker's inability to locate his reserved *Amateur Photographer* magazine. At length, he angrily suggested how an overhaul of the shop's subscription service protocols might work. Those queuing behind him sighed and stared listlessly at their phones, wondering whether lockdown would be such a bad thing after all. 'I really have had enough of this year,' said a man in his twenties, 'I really have.'

I'd popped into Smith's to try and find a local history book. 'During the medieval period Kendal was subject to famine, Scottish raids, and bad harvests', said one; yet again, history's grim tidings were suggesting that things could be worse, surely the default position of our national psyche. In that era, the book – *Secret Kendal* by Andrew Graham Stables – continued, this town had been famed for its production of cheap tough cotton. Much of the rag worn by paupers in London and elsewhere had originated here, a claim to fame of sorts, and the town's Latin motto – *Pannus mihi panis* – translates as 'Wool is my bread'. Indeed, in William Shakespeare's *Henry IV, Part I*, Falstaff remarks: 'But as the Devil would have it, three misbegotten knaves in Kendal green came at my back.'

Idling on Finkle Street, a scattering of tourists made the most of things – 'Christ knows when we'll get away again,' said one dad, sanctioning the purchase of a mega-sized Romney's Kendal Mint Cake with an air of Last Days of Rome largesse. Some paused to look at the Kendal Snake Trail, a collection of hand-painted rocks. 'In 2020', read an accompanying plaque, 'our community came together during a global pandemic, one painted pebble at a time.' 'They'll be needing more bloody pebbles soon,' offered a middle-aged woman in a wolf-patterned fleece jacket.

On a bench outside the striking old Working Men's Institute – To Let and in a state of destitution – I ate a pasty and wondered if my season's journey was about to end. Only seven weeks had passed since the sunlit uplands of Jarrow. The future some of us fools had allowed ourselves to look to back then had been subverted. Football fixtures seemed to be fading from the card once more, like names on a weather-beaten old gravestone.

Down by the Kent, a broad river that today seemed to frolic and swirl rather than run in any particular direction, grandads tried to impress with skimmers and their grandkids made the case for ice cream or home time. By the tea rooms and crooked lodgings of Highgate, I made my way towards Parkside Road. Outside shops and on corners, people had stopped to share rumours and fears. They spoke in the language they did not wish to, but that we had all acquired since March, as if we were a nation under occupation by some foreign power – lockdown and furlough, vaccine trials and second waves, quarantine and self-isolation, track and trace and all the rest. For two sacred hours I was about to shed that dialect and lose myself in football. It increasingly felt like the only language I truly understood.

* * *

From the raised pavement opposite, you could see them. A dozen or so followers of Kendal Town, gathered for what they knew, deep down, would be the last occasion on which Saturday, 3pm meant something significant until an unknowable point in the future. Although each week the big hand may still fix on 12 and the small on three, it would once again melt into a commonplace point in the clock, just like any other. They stood on an old stub of terrace, clapping their hands together to keep warm and staring straight ahead to the pitch. This was a time for brave faces, just like those minutes before a parent takes their child off to university or drops them at an airport. Every season has its last fixture, but usually supporters could count the days until the next one. In the uncertainty of the present and in recalling the previous lockdown, this felt like an unlimited sentence without parole.

Being above the Parkside Road ground like this granted it the presence of a hobbyist's amphitheatre. It was possible to see its various homely sheds and outbuildings and its liver-spotted corrugated roofs. Discarded pillars poked out from overgrown patches of grass and piles of leaves like forgotten periscopes. There was even an intricate old turnstile, standing quite alone in the manner of someone waiting to be asked for a dance. The only thing missing was a pottering grandad with a mug of tea in one hand and a spanner in the other.

At the one turnstile that still had dance partners, a father and son queued ahead of me. 'Can we go behind the goal this time?' asked the child. 'Course we can,' replied his dad. The boy did a celebratory little hop and it occurred to me that the size of a stadium and the level of a football match hardly matters when you are nine and allowed to stand listening to a goalkeeper swearing. As they paid their money, dad urged son to 'Say thank you to The Man' and I thought back to what a big presence 'The Man' was during childhood – a parent and their 'I'm going to say something to The Man' when other kids were talking in the cinema, or an 'I'm telling The Man' from one youngster to a misbehaving other at the swimming baths. Woe betide us all when that dreaded alarm call of 'The Man's coming!' was sounded. I paid my money and thanked The Man.

'Track and Trace over there if you don't mind, sir,' came the cheery – and distinctly 2020 – greeting once I was through. I wrote down my details on a form that rested upon a table I hoped was more usually deployed for 'new signing' photographs. If so, then it was the closest I'd ever come to featuring in one, unless Tadcaster announced that they were short of a left-back. Mind, pushing 40, even the age-old dream of a hapless assistant manager appealing among the crowd for a player and picking me had gone into retirement. Now, I fantasised about being chosen to watch a match from the warmth of an executive box or just being awarded some really decent gloves.

The signing took place in Parkside Road's cow shed enclosure, a two-stepped terrace whose car-port-style pillars enhanced the ground's grandpa DIY charm. In front of the stand, a small Lakeland tarn had formed, with a single orange traffic cone placed at its centre. This lent the scene the air of a team challenge at a particularly shabby outdoor retreat. It also seemed like an apt visual metaphor: season 2020/21, proceed with caution.

The cow shed's roof, in common with every wall and barrier here, was painted in broad black-and-white stripes, echoing the team's shirts. Through much of the game, this decoration was to catch my eye and remind me of the tiny rolling graphic that used to appear on ITV programmes when an advertisement break was about to begin. I half expected to see one of the home team's attacks brought to an abrupt halt while a message about how the ambassador's receptions were 'noted in society for their host's exquisite taste' was read out over the public address system.

At five to three, the sky stopped weeping and a pale kind of sunshine transpired. There was no raging against the dying of the light, but such jaded embers seemed apt for this season and for everything we were living through. Uncertainty had made us, and football, weary.

Yet even in the final moments before a kick-off we presumed would be the last for some months, distraction and energy were there if you looked. Joy, even. In the centre circle, referee Nathaniel Cox attempted keepy-uppies but lost control of the ball spectacularly. Members of both squads laughed like schoolchildren whose teacher had fallen over. Then, on the terrace behind a goal, 40 or so teenage boys swarmed together and began to chant with hedonistic exuberance. 'Oh when the Town/Go marching in…' they sang throatily and with grotty, raw emotion. 'Who are we?' gnarled their leader. 'Town army!' came the choir's answer. Discovering these young bawlers amid the peace and prettiness of the Lake District was like finding punk in an opera house; I loved it. The boys of the Westmorland curva were a reminder that whatever happened next, football would someday bloom again and bloom bright.

Many of their voices had not yet broken. They adopted the tactic of faking along, forcing bass tones from somewhere deep in the throat like Grange Hill kids trying to buy cider in Safeway. They needn't have worried – a throbbing drum underpinned much of the din. It was enough to ward off any evil Halloween spirit and even to drown out those men around me who insisted on updating anyone nearby on rumoured events from the dastardly real world outside: 'Oh, Boris's doing a press conference at half four' and 'That'll be it for the pubs'. Where once the scores from matches elsewhere rumbled around alone, they were now accompanied by whispers of circuit breakers and home-schooling. Still they spoke of team news and players gone by, but such sad tidings were interspersed among their happy ramblings. Covid had breached the turnstiles.

One hundred and one years ago, the Mintcakes had been founded by workers of the Netherfield shoe factory and taken its name as their own. Keen on a fit and healthy workforce – perhaps in reaction to the grisly catastrophes of World War One – the company gave Netherfield FC an adjacent plot of land to call home. Parkfield Road would outlast the factory; shoemaking in Kendal ceased in 2003. Jarrow ships, Teesside steel, Workington rails, Kendal shoes… to tour Britain in the 21st century is to walk in the past tense among remnants of what was.

Their most famous brand had been K Shoes. In 1913, 230,000 pairs a year were being made at Netherfield's; a year later, its staff manufactured marching boots and leather leggings for the French and Russian armed forces. At one time, 20 per cent of the town's working-age population were employed in the factory. Elsewhere, such industrial prowess was enough on which to construct some form of footballing success. Netherfield, though, had rarely scaled higher than their current billing as the renamed Kendal Town in the eighth tier of English football, drifting along in the West Lancashire League and the Lancashire Combination, among others.

Their fate could, perhaps, have twisted in a more bounteous direction had they signed the teenager they had taken on trial in the late 1930s, Tom Finney. Instead, he was rejected for being too slight. Finney's brother, Joe, became a Netherfield regular, playing on over 200 occasions. Sir Tom, meanwhile, happily accepted an official apology from the club for his rejection, along with the position of President, in 2007. Discarding Finney, said chairman David Willan, had been 'The biggest mistake in football history'. Like Shankly at Workington, the man who became known as the Preston Plumber had a lounge bar named after him within the team's ground.

Finney or not, there were dalliances in the cups along the way, including ties in the first and second rounds of the FA Cup, and then calamitously in the FA Trophy of 1980/81. That year, Netherfield and Bridlington Trinity achieved an unwanted record, drawing six times in the competition's first round, until, after 13-and-a-half hours of stalemate, the Mintcakes emerged 2-0 victors in a seventh match. This mammoth entanglement cost

Netherfield thousands of pounds – money they could ill afford – and scything cuts had to be made. By 1982/83, they had floundered and then withered. That season saw them concede 129 goals – the most they ever had done – and win only twice, gathering a mere 15 points. Only league reconstruction reversed the wretched trend; in 1987, structural changes awarded Netherfield a return to the Northern Premier League. At the millennium's turn, with K Shoes increasingly a nostalgic memory, Netherfield changed their name to Kendal Town.

* * *

The black-and-white-shirted herd trampled over – five or six Kendal players, all huddled and awaiting the ball straight from kick-off. Nathaniel Cox whistled, Mintcakes winger Jamie Hodgson rolled the ball backwards to teammate Jordan Scott and he loafed it over the heads of the entire congregation and out of play. 'Bloody hell, Kendal,' said a man near me, and then 'Bloody hell' again, while shaking his head.

When they kept the ball within the confines of the pitch, his team imposed themselves on Tadcaster, irritating them into mistakes. Soaring Mintcakes forward Hugo Rodríguez seemed to buttonhole his marker, Ioan Evans, preventing him from carrying the ball out of defence. It was like watching a particularly relentless charity worker accosting someone in the street. As a teenager, Rodríguez had captained the Sevilla youth team, playing alongside Sergio Ramos. Savage fortune, though, robbed him of a high-level career – a persistent injury forced retirement from the professional game. Such subplots and *what if?* tales of woe can be found throughout football down in the trenches.

Each time players migrated close to the sideline, their stampeding feet made sploshing, pitter-patter melodies in the sodden turf. It sounded as if ballet were being performed in a sheep dip. Added to this oddly therapeutic composition was the rustling of leaves in those parts of the pitch overshadowed by shedding trees. On several occasions, a defender clouted the ball clear and found he had also inadvertently summoned a shooting star of russet, amber and ochre, like some autumnal magician. Or a sudden gale would conjure a leaf whirlwind around a winger as he dribbled forward. The only thing missing from the scene was a goalkeeper challenging a full-back to a game of conkers.

In the penalty area, Rodríguez accosted Evans one too many times and Cox gave a free-kick. 'You're not fit to referee' sang the Mintcake ultras. A haunting of smoke swelled by the corner flag and I wondered if they had set off a flare. Investigation demonstrated otherwise, however. Instead, the plume was rising from a rusty fire barrel of the type usually seen on picket lines. Its presence enriched the feeling that everything beyond the pitch at Parkside Road was the domain of a pottering old man, who possibly lived beneath the stand. It wasn't clear exactly what was being burned, though a faint tar scent mingled with the fumes.

In the Tadcaster Albion dugout, the coaching staff worked through a lexicon of commands. 'On his toes!' and 'Box him in!' were followed by 'Name it!', 'Round the corner!' and 'Work it!' One of the terrifying things about consuming so much football is that you inhale these utterings and begin to understand them. Other humans pick up some passable French while on holiday or a smattering of Mandarin from a Chinese friend; followers of this game come to learn exactly what 'First to the second' and 'Line it' mean. It is useless and yet uniting, an Esperanto of the turf.

Those Albion coaches were momentarily silenced when the linesman sloshed by in front of them, causing a swampy tidal wave that threatened to submerge their trainers. Each man looked down at his feet and seemed to spend a few moments questioning his life choices. Penalty box happenings snapped them from their trances when Rodríguez apparently used his hand to manufacture a chance on goal, which he then missed in any case. 'Handball!' came the stereo cries. Again, the linesman hurtled by, forcing the men to crouch quickly backwards as if hiding from a bully in a hedge. 'I'm the linesman, not you!' he yelled as he went past, in case there was any doubt.

With 20 minutes elapsed, Kendal seemed to tire. Their midfield appeared bloated and drowsy, as if on a night out together and considering a round of espresso martinis to engineer 'a second wind'. The Brewers began to spark, calculating how to play passing football on a dense bog in the manner of a chameleon adapting to its surroundings. Confidence blossomed into attempts on Morgan Bacon's Kendal goal. Midfielder Simon Russell, whose pale ginger hair had absorbed rainwater and now resembled the dishevelled mane of a lost baby giraffe, struck a particularly shapely howitzer his way. The Kendal goalkeeper sailed through the air like a ghost at clocking-off time and clawed the ball over. 'Morgan Bacon,' sang the ultras, 'he's coming for you.'

The Albion blitz continued, revolving around right-back James Ngoe and the electric young winger ahead of him, Ify Ofoegbu. Together they pulverised the Kendal left, weaving triangles and leaving their opponents panting as if they were movie felons cornered in a chase. One such manoeuvre won their side a penalty.

In the curva nord, 20 teenagers clustered behind the goal to pester Russell, the penalty taker. When he placed the ball on the spot and stepped backwards, they waved their arms as if lost at sea and made wanker signs in the sky like bedevilled conductors. Through Russell's run-up there came a jeer that reached its crescendo when he struck the ball. This pantomime act, performed before opposition penalties for so many years now, is the very opposite of Corinthian sporting values and is tremendously enjoyable to watch.

Bacon saved low to his left. More young fans joined those at the front in celebration, gig-goers rushing forward for their favourite song. It was hard to imagine much else that made teenagers so exultantly happy. A minute or two later, something happened that did: a brawl.

It began when Bacon saved at point-blank range and was then fouled. As he sprawled on the ground, a Brewers player blasted the ball into his body. It acted as a lightning bolt, spurring him to life and on to his feet. A pile-on followed, with nearly every man on the pitch tussling and throttling. 'G'wan,' roared a man near me. 'This is why we're here!' said his friend. 'Come away, come away,' flowed the advice from the Albion bench. 'Morgan Bacon/He's coming for you,' bayed the ultras. In view of distant Lakeland mountains and in the middle of gentle old Kendal town, it all seemed incongruous – the pretty cottage with a big bad wolf waiting inside. Perhaps the febrile outside world with its lock-down murmurs had made it over the white line too.

With relative peace asserted, the game plunged into a rut of familiarity. Albion would push the ball around with courage and invention, and their hosts hoist it forward for Rodríguez to chase. It was as if he was a child they were trying to exhaust before the babysitter arrived. Towards half-time, the Spaniard began to lunge towards goal-kicks winched his way with the low shoulders and bent neck of a condemned man on his way to the gallows.

Then, just before the whistle, Albion passed their way through the quagmire and Ofoegbu advanced clear with the ball. 'Make them pay!' yapped a teammate in a high-pitched West Yorkshire voice that made it sound more irked market-stall holder than vengeful gangster. Ofoegbu arrowed the ball into the net for 1-0. He and half a dozen comrades ran to the corner and celebrated on a carpet of spent leaves, their yellow shirts and socks harmonising.

In Finney's Sports Bar, some queued and others gazed through windows on to the vacant half-time pitch. A bobble-hatted couple nuzzled and a mum cradled her baby. Two or three old men on their own stared forward impassively. One looked across and asked of another, 'You going next week, Nigel?' The man turned slowly and replied only with a shrug of his shoulders. He knew now that it was not up to him. Lockdown déjà vu was an unsettling, oppressive sensation. I bought a bar of Romney's Kendal Mint Cake and went for a wander to pretend the fretful feeling in my stomach could be cured with sugar and fresh air.

Up beyond the terrace, in an area I now firmly thought of as Grandad's Corner, there was a peaceful netherworld of the disused. The stand-alone ironwork turnstile stood on a concrete plinth looking out to the pitch and then the mountains beyond. It was as if for a retirement gift they had allowed it to watch some of the action it had for so long heard about but been sheltered from. This was the discarded turnstile's version of a retirement home with sea views. At its base, the pedal an operator would formerly push with his or her foot protruded lifeless and untouched for years, a high five left forever hanging.

Down below, moss grasped at a roofless brick Gents toilet block that was at least half a century old and now cordoned off. Ticker tape and a single police cone blocked one end, a rusting trolley cart the other. In the graveyard behind, birds jabbered. For a while I tried to decipher a painted-over sign pinned on the old main stand but became distracted by a tiny wooden door beneath. Either I'd found Grandad's cubbyhole home, or Halloween was getting to me.

Through the early portions of the second half, Kendal pressed forward in a gradualist, furtive way. Their midfield had now found droplets of energy, but each man moved in the wary fashion of a person tasked with sniffing milk close to its 'use by' date. It appeared that they were afraid of what they might find in the penalty area.

Eventually, Jamie Hodgson – who with his high-and-tight cut and untucked shirt had the look of a 1950s GI on leave – seemed to ladle his foot around the ball and scoop it into the box. Rodríguez admirably propelled himself in its direction but ended up prone in the leaves like an abandoned scarecrow. 'We love you/ We love you/We love you,' crooned the ultras. Shortly afterwards, Emil Jääskeläinen, the striker's partner, somehow urged the ball into the net from another Hodgson loop across goal. Everything good frittered to dust: the linesman decreed Jääskeläinen offside, Kendal cheers disintegrated, and a severely enraged teenager scrambled down the terrace to shout 'YOU JOBSWORTH SHITBAG' at the referee.

The sun slowly collapsed and in front of the Brewers dugout, Kévin dos Santos, a 21-year-old Portuguese lately of Setúbal Vitória, unzipped his tracksuit. The substitute received his instructions, had his studs checked and jogged on to the turf. Sometimes it appears as if a footballer knows that he is about to play wonderfully or win a match all on his own. It is in his swagger and his earliest acts. This was one of those moments. Kendal had been pressing for an equaliser; dos Santos's first hip swivel and darting run was a declaration that they may as well surrender now.

There were spins and twirls, shots curled artfully on to the bar and pulsating changes in pace. At one point, he seemed to make the ball heel and then loyally dash with him into the box as if we were watching master and dog at Cruft's. Soon a slalom run and rolled cross let striker Bailey Thompson tap in for 0-2.

The Brewers' perfect third goal began with a back pass to their goalkeeper, Will Appleyard. His ball out of defence was the earliest of a dozen unbroken passes, many made first time. In a matter of seconds, on a taxing pitch and among gathering winds, they had stroked their way impulsively from box to box. This pincer movement's executioner, Simon Russell, stepped his way around Morgan Bacon as if the keeper was a boulder in a stream, and scored.

Still the ultras banged their drum and sang of following the Mintcakes 'Cos that's the way we like it'. When an errant shot ended up among them, they threw the ball around and cheered. 'It's your time you're wasting,' said Appleyard as he stood in front of them, teacher and class. Perhaps they knew what was coming and just did not want this game to end. Leaves swelled around Appleyard when finally he took his goal-kick and soon afterwards the full-time whistle sounded.

'Our next home game is against Clitheroe in a fortnight's time,' came an announcement over the public address system. Two hours later, the prime minister declared that very soon England would return to lockdown. Attending a football match was once again impossible. They weren't singing any more.

5

05/12/20
Southport 1 v 1 Alfreton Town
National League North

In Lancaster and in Workington, in Kendal and in Jarrow, and in a thousand towns whose teams simply could not play without gate money, football once more drifted off into hibernation. Higher up the chain, television revenues and other subsidies allowed behind-closed-doors matches to amble on just as they had all season. Professional football remained a gated community.

The idea of turnstiles creaking and catering hatches being unfurled receded and became fantastical. All supporters could do was draw on memory and try to summon optimism, though that seemed to ebb and flicker dimly as if surviving on limp batteries. Across all these isles – locked down or languishing in various levels of restriction – and beyond anything to do with football, November was the cruellest month. Hope rested in science – a first Covid vaccine was approved – and blind faith in political promises; Christmas, we were told, would be just like the good old days with family house visits, wanted or otherwise.

Early in December, England's second lockdown ended. As in the autumn, a system of regional restrictions was implemented, with each local authority placed in a numbered tier. There existed the opportunity to move around these divisions according to

Covid case numbers, a bleak kind of promotion and relegation. Vague caveats and subclauses abounded – pubs that served 'substantial meals' could remain open, unlike purely 'wet' pubs. What a substantial meal constituted led to a very British debate about the nutritional benefits of Scotch eggs.

Though many non-professional leagues were suspended, a number of local cup competitions continued. Some leftovers from the curtailed 2019/20 season ran alongside their 2020/21 versions. It caused the same kind of timeline bewilderment as watching *Back to the Future II* after a night out.

In those weeks between the lockdown sequel and Christmas, clubs staging such games pondered whether their bars could be opened on matchdays to let tills ring, with pies – or Scotch eggs – served. Fans could, perhaps, watch the action from the windows of those club bars or their beer garden benches. It seemed like a resolution of sorts, even if it had become clear that being indoors was far more dangerous for Covid transmission than standing outside on a terrace. Though officially frowned upon, at some social clubs vertical blinds twitched with prying eyes and grown men watched games through fence cracks. Football seeped through.

In tandem, there existed directly sanctioned ways to spectate. Matches staged in places living under the lowest restrictions were permitted fans in the ground. Higher up in England, crowds ranging from a few hundred to a couple of thousand were allowed for some matches in the Premier League, Football League and National League.

These yuletide fixtures in the professional game represented everything that those fortunate enough to obtain tickets had been waiting for. It was nine months since they last walked their pilgrim routes and sat in those seats they considered their own. Their advent calendars had reached day 266 and now it was time to go home.

There was genuine, romantic optimism – always more possible when the Christmas trees are up – that these were the first acts of a storyline that would end with every supporter across the land returning to their rightful place. However, as had been the case in October, those watching did so while menaced by the intrusive, irrepressible thought that each game could be the last for some time. Every day, Covid cases, hospitalisations and deaths grew. It was hard to think of lockdown as something from the past. Most of us now saw it as some looming spectre always hiding in wait around a dangerous corner.

Nonetheless, five weeks after the doomsday feel of a Kendal Town Halloween, to stand on a terrace again would be a reprieve and an unexpected pleasure. Even football watched on borrowed time offers escape and delight. It was time to head for the Paris of the North.

* * *

On the train from Wigan Wallgate, I lost myself watching back gardens flicker by. Each offered fleeting, zoetrope glimpses into the lives of people I'd never meet. There were crooked trampolines, orderly sheds and greenhouses with ball-shaped scars, and there were ragged St George flags on masts higher than rooftops, mini goals that had fallen over and an enormous, stagnant hot tub. Some gardens were shabby, most tended and loved, or at least cheerful through being played in.

Through Gathurst, Appley Bridge, Parbold and Hoscar, I reflected how 2020 had made lives lived in disparate towns, villages and gardens so remarkably similar. Our liberties and our options of existence and entertainment had been closed down as one. There was a dark democracy to what had happened. Now, most people were united again by a shared fear that sounded like the threatening premise of a Disney movie: that Christmas might be cancelled.

At Burscough Bridge, two middle-aged ladies boarded and sat behind me. They indulged in a stream of chatter as only close friends or family members can; no explanations of persons or people mentioned were needed, topics revolved with not a breath in between and it seemed that very few recent events were unimportant enough to be omitted. 'Thanks for that mulled wine by the way, lovey. Did I tell you about the coconut sugar? No? So, I gets this text from school saying our James needs to bake a cake. I try every shop in town. Nowt...'

Alongside the shabby old train's whines and grunts, this chatter became another layer of unremitting sound. Clanking, shrieking wheels were the drumbeat, and monologues about dreams and herbal tea the bassline. Yet so easily can the fickle football devotee be won over that any festering irritation was swept away when one of them spoke the words: 'I am missing going to Wigan matches. I love it. Even if they don't score, I just love it.'

We choked through Bescar Lane, the comely rural station that John Lennon used when labouring on a nearby building site in Scarisbrick through the summer of 1959. One morning, the future Beatle failed to put water into a tea boiler that usually slaked the thirst of the site's navvies. The empty boiler burned dangerously and broke. There was a minor riot and Lennon was sacked for being 'unsuitable'. He didn't care: the job had earned him enough money for his first electric guitar.

Southport, ten minutes down the line, has long had such Liverpool connections. It has been to many Liverpudlians a beloved summer holiday town and somewhere those Scousers who 'got on' or 'did alright for themselves' moved to. Today, duckling-yellow Merseyrail carriages lined the train station's platforms and Southport Football Club could allow spectators because their town was part of the Tier Two Liverpool City region.

Though talk of a lost and lonely Christmas growled on, Southport town centre laboured hard to ignore it. A Salvation Army band bloated out carols and people anchored down by plastic bags queued outside shops. By the store she worked in, a woman having a cigarette told a colleague that she would 'chop my own ears off if I have to hear Noddy Holder one more chuffing time'. Then an exasperated wife berated her husband for taking no interest in her present-buying plans and everything felt reassuringly normal.

A great obelisk drew me along London Road and on to Lord Street. It was one of three war memorials posing gallantly, the other two being colonnades with the charisma of Greek temples on either side of it, commas surrounding an exclamation mark. Something changed in the sky above and one of them was suddenly smeared with incandescent sunlight, as if God had beamed His bedside lamp on it. This blaze illuminated an inscription – 'Tell Britain, Ye Who Mark This Monument:' – that appeared to be an unfinished sentence left hanging. Its conclusion was around the other side – 'Faithful To Her We Fell And Rest Content'. Such words will always move us but in 2020 they again reminded us this: there have been worse times.

Lord Street is this town's finest, and among the most elegant in England. Trees queue on wide pavement edges as if waiting for the bus, and for half a mile cast-iron canopies droop from buildings like luscious eyelids. Locals will tell you that this boulevard inspired Louis-Napoléon Bonaparte and Baron Haussmann's remodelling of Paris through the 1850s. Exiled from France, Louis-Napoléon had stayed here in 1846 and apparently been captivated by what he saw. I was bewitched, too, firstly by the faded magnificence of Lord Street's old hotels, and then by Antonio's ice cream parlour, a joyous corner house of giant fibreglass 99s, bagged candyflosses dangling from hooks like friendly punchbags and busy kaleidoscope counters of rock and hard-boiled dummy necklaces. Queuing for an ice cream, a man spoke wistfully to his daughter. 'They used to put jokes on ice lolly sticks, you know,' he said, 'then it stopped.' 'Why did it stop?' she asked. 'I don't know, love,' he replied, and then muttered another 'I don't know' with an added, slow shake of the head. He stared into the ice-cream cabinet and possibly into the past too.

A left turn from Lord Street transplanted me to seaside England, the place I often wish to be. The vapours of doughnuts, chips and other deep-fried wonders frolicked in the air. Neon lights above the doors of amusement arcades flashed and flickered, badgering those who passed by until eventually they fumbled in their pockets for coins and staggered inside. Out from those arcades' doors were flung the chirps and sirens of their machines. They competed with the merry organ tones of a beautiful old carousel named Herbert Silcock's Original Superb Parade of All British Galloping Horses. Its decorated wooden equines undulated like a gentle morning tide, which was just as well because this seaside town's ocean is often almost invisible.

Southport's tide has withdrawn as if disinterested. Blackpool Tower is visible from here, and the visitor might wonder if the sea has been seduced by that place's bawdier charms. It wasn't always so. During the 19th century, a town grew from a village as tourists began visiting to bathe in the Irish Sea. Then, largely in the Victorian era, it began to retreat, so that now waves can only be closely watched by standing at the end of Southport Pier. The sea no longer visits you, so you must visit it as if it is an incapacitated relative in a home.

Southport did not mourn the backwards march of its ocean. The lands left by the tide's escape represented an opportunity. Where engineering could be calculated, pleasure was installed in the form of fair rides and Pierrot theatre shows. Where the land was too marshy and sodden to be built upon, a broad and happy boating lake, still here today, was established.

The voids were filled with joy. High above the lake, a cableway strung between two grand towers flew passengers in gondolas across its length. There were helter-skelters, a gargantuan water chute and Maxim's Captive Flying Machine, a daring contraption that scooted riders through the air in primitive Edwardian spaceships. From 1920, the Giro Aviation Company offered biplane pleasure flights along the beach and to Blackpool. Three years later, Southport's sea had become so shallow that the steamboats that once chugged holidaymakers to the pier jetty from Liverpool, Wales and beyond could sail no more. The future seemed to be in the sky. Later, the foreign package vacations that elbowed seaside towns from the map proved that all over again.

Those days of flying machines fizzled along through times of vaulting ambition and scant regard for personal safety. Now,

Funland – with its name painted in strident rosy lettering on a white wall that looked delicious against today's rich blue sky – offered 'Family Fun from 2p to £1. Why Pay More?' A side entrance took customers inside the Hall of Mirrors ('FREE' it boasted on three separate occasions), with distorted caricatures of Laurel and Hardy in each window and on its awning. Perhaps Laurel and Hardy knew why these places are always called a 'hall', and never a 'room' or, as would often be more accurate, a 'cupboard'.

Inside Funland, the arcade orchestra gave its usual calamitous and buoyant performance. All the familiar instruments were there. Tuppence coins fell into collection trays in dribs and drabs like a slow pipe leak. Change machines rained their 10 pence pieces into plastic pots, a shrill deluge. Fruit machines warbled, bleeped tunefully and then let out electronic sighs when jack-pots were not won. Every 30 seconds, Whittaker's Gold Cup, an updated version of the traditional automatic horse-racing game, made its robotic announcements of 'The winner... Number two... White Rose... Ridden by...' A hundred other machines trilled and cheeped their themes and catchphrases, competing and yet, somehow, never talking over one another. It was, alto-gether, an assault and yet every bit as enlivening and enriching as bracing sea air.

Nevertheless, I walked to the pier's end. At any seaside, this is always an oddly solemn experience after the hedonism of an esplanade, but surreally so with no water beneath. Huge, empty and gorgeous skies lifted everything, as did a close view at last of the Irish Sea. When Southport Pier had a slightly longer reach, and when the ocean strayed further inwards, this was the site of Thom's Tea House. From its roof, a derring-do troupe called the Professors would jump 40 feet into the water. Sometimes, the Professors rode bicycles straight in, or dived while on fire or tied up in a sack. In their hundreds, people paid to watch.

Back at the Esplanade, I paused and read a tarpaulin banner fixed to a fence by the local council. 'It's not forever', it said, 'Keep Social Distancing.' How we longed for a day when these messages were neither seen nor heard, a time when all this was a faint and sickly memory. And how we longed to believe that this really wasn't forever.

Nearby, a boy of eight or nine raised a foot as if he was about to climb on the railings. 'God, Josh,' grumbled his dad from a few metres away, 'how many times have I told you not to do that? Stay still.' Beneath us all on the temporary stage outside a pub, a waist-coated pensioner who possibly saw himself as 'still a bit of a hit with The Ladies' sang Christmas hits into a karaoke machine. During a particularly comatose rendition of 'White Christmas', the man pleaded 'Right, over to you...' and held his microphone to the audience – a woman sitting facing the other way with her dog. The boy ran speedily away. 'Stop, Josh! Bloody hell, lad. Have you got glue ear or summat?' said his dad, but I thought Josh had the right idea.

* * *

There was not time to visit the British Lawnmower Museum and so I pressed on towards the ground. Though they might be tree-lined and benign, some streets are relentless to walk and feel as though you are proceeding gloopily, as if walking the wrong way on an airport travelator. Such was the case with the mile-long trek along Scarisbrick New Road, where houses seemed to repeat each other in the manner of a crushingly boring drunk. Then on a corner stood a family in yellow-and-black-striped scarves, human weathervanes pointing towards a break in the monotony.

I walked past them and into Haig Avenue, the street on which Southport play and that their ground is named after. Beyond smart gardens with monkey puzzle trees and yet more pave-ment poplars, floodlight pylons beckoned. Strolls accelerated into scampers and people dared to smile and rub their hands together in astonishment. Here we were, back invading the turn-stiles, an act that had seemed impossibly distant only a fortnight ago. Outside the club shop, masked men queued two metres apart, ready to turn Christmas black and yellow. 'Did you have a good lockdown, John?' called one to another. 'Yeah, not bad.

How was yours?' 'Oh you know, quiet,' he replied, at which point they erupted in laughter. It had become the new 'How was your holiday?' or 'What are you doing for Christmas?', and an outlet for the blackest of humours. Behind them, supporters gathered by the main stand. Its side profile resembled some form of giant and grinning shark, with panes of Perspex gleaming in the sunlight like expectant teeth.

By a red-brick entrance block, the script was the same every time. Each supporter that arrived looked ahead and around, grinned and then fixed on their face mask. Then, they disappeared into the dim hollow and all that could be known of them was the 'cheers' or the 'thanks, mate' that came next, and the dislocated clanks of the turnstiles joining in the conversation.

This town has had its club since those days of magnificent Victorians and their flying machines. 'Football is looking up in the pleasant seaport whose only defect is being without the sea,' claimed *Athletic News* in 1888, seven years after the team soon known as the Sandgrounders first played.

Often in a place of tourism, though, money visits and floats around seafronts and attractions, rarely finding its way to football coffers; Southport's were barren from the off. During the 1895/96 season, posters were placed around town asking, in reference to the impoverished club, 'Shall It Die?' The appeal cultivated attention and galvanised fundraising. One committee member donated a fox terrier puppy as a raffle prize, raising £18 for the cause. The Sandgrounders were saved, but crises of existence followed by preservation campaigns became a regular pattern for the next century.

In that time there were periods of note and tragedy, intrigue and desperation. For a year at the end of World War One, the club was taken over by a motor car company and renamed in its honour as Southport Vulcan, the first such commercial designation for a team. In 1921, the Sandgrounders were elected for the first time to the Football League, joining Division Three (North) in its maiden season. Three years later, with his team top of the league, 22-year-old inside-left Peter Mee went walking by the Mersey on a foggy Guy Fawkes night and was never seen again. 'FOOTBALLER FOUND DROWNED' and 'FOOTBALLER'S BODY IN RIVER' read the terrible headlines six weeks later.

Though football must not have mattered much to friends, teammates and followers of young Mee for some time, club life rumbled on. The 1930/31 season was one of Southport's finest – an immense FA Cup run saw victories against Millwall, Blackpool and Bradford Park Avenue, with 17,500 people inside Haig Avenue for the latter. As if shaking off delusions of grandeur, the team found themselves 7-0 down inside 42 minutes of their quarter-final tie with Everton, eventually losing 9-1.

Success was an oddity. The Sandgrounders' default existence was one of financial grief and low-table finishes. Each glum placing left them scrambling for enough votes from other clubs to be re-elected to the Football League. Then from 1966 unfolded a dozen years of turbulence laced with moments and enterprises that now seem bleakly amusing, to the uninitiated and unconnected at least.

First came some rare glee. In 1965, the club appointed Northern Irishman Billy Bingham as manager. His worship of fitness and organisation and his direct, muscular interpretation of the game combined to win promotion, Southport's first ever in league football, during 1966/67. Defying expectation and a history of malaise, the Sandgrounders stayed up in Division Three. Then came a modest miracle: an eighth-place finish in 1968/69. It would be their highest ever position.

Relegation visited the following term, barging Southport back into what many thought of as their rightful place. There did follow a further, single season in elevated company by virtue of a Division Four title win in 1973, but soon doom and farce enveloped the club. Most of it was cast down from the bungling boardroom.

In the relegation summer of 1974, new chairman Tom Robinson pledged to reach for the moon on what turned out to be a fairground ride budget. Fan folklore still holds today that a hire purchase company repossessed Robinson's Rolls-Royce from the Haig Avenue car park as he watched a match from the directors' box.

During the summer of 1975, Southport commercial manager Albert Dunlop undertook some grand planning of his own. His great idea was to raise funds by bringing razzmatazz to Haig Avenue. An advert headline in the local press proclaimed the scheme: 'POP FESTIVAL 75'. On 26 July, 12,000 people would pay to watch 'The North's Biggest 1-Day Pop Festival' from the pitch and terraces. Showaddywaddy were to headline, with sets too from Quiver, Fogg and more overwhelmingly 1970s acts. 'The show will be compered by disc jockey Billy Butler', reported the *Liverpool Echo*.

The stage was set. However, Showaddywaddy and Geno Washington & the Ram Jam Band refused to walk on, pulling out of Pop Festival 75 the day before it was due to begin. 'There has been some trouble over the contracts,' said Dunlop, 'but I am not prepared to discuss this as it is a matter between myself and the groups.'

An audience of only 1,000 people attended the reduced event. 'NO MORE POP AFTER FESTIVAL FLOP' ran the *Echo*'s headline the following Monday. 'Pop festivals are definitely out,' commented Dunlop. 'The poor turnout was a hefty blow for both the club and myself. I feel very disheartened.' He denied that tickets had been overpriced and rounded on locals for their lack of support, claiming that only 2 per cent of attendees had been from Southport. Soon after, Dunlop was suspended from work.

Though a team can strive for happenings beyond the touchline not to affect playing matters, it is usually impossible. Boardroom and management buffoonery seems to filter its way to the dugout and the penalty area, resulting in feeble performances and abject results. The dreary cycle is complete when that same board then clumsily intervenes in an attempt to steady matters on the field. So it was with Southport in 1975/76, the term that began days after Showaddywaddy's no-show.

Early in the season, the Sandgrounders lost 11 matches in succession and were stranded at the foot of Division Four. Chairman Tom Robinson responded by recruiting a hypnotist named Romark to cure the team's ills. Five players attended a hypnosis session with Romark in the hours prior to a Tuesday evening home fixture with Watford. One of them, Kevin Thomas, emerged from Romark's spell and thwacked his head on an iron girder beneath Haig Avenue's main stand. Thomas required stitches. He was Southport's goalkeeper, and conceded within three minutes of kick-off. The team lost again, 1-2.

Romark claimed his hypnosis would continue to offer enchantment into the following Saturday's game with Crewe Alexandra. A draw finally stopped the rot, though whether the hypnotist can be credited is debatable. Later in the season, he claimed to have put a curse on Malcolm Allison's Crystal Palace after they failed to pay his invoice for psychic services rendered.

Southport finished second bottom that year. Only Workington were below them. In 1976/77, cardboard league ladder tabs were left in place across the land; the two contrived to finish in exactly the same dreaded positions. Workington were finally voted out of the Football League, as we have seen. The following year, the Sandgrounders finished in their customary berth – 23rd of 24 teams. This time, Rochdale propped them up. Amid the usual background shenanigans and rumours of back-stabbing, grudges and bribery through boardroom buffets, Southport were voted out of the league. Like Workington, they would never return.

*   *   *

After scattergun turnstile melodies came the grenades of footballs being punted by goalkeeping coaches and their subjects. Some of their crosses and kicks skedaddled into Haig Avenue's three sides of orderly terracing. The balls bounced between steps like slinkies before being retrieved by some child or other and propelled back to the pitch. Each little boy or girl that performed this task turned and beamed to mum or dad. They had touched the ball and would not forget it. This game sprinkles the simplest and most memorable gifts on those who love it. Anywhere else, a ball is just a ball. In a football ground, it is treasure.

Standing on an open-air terrace that ran the length of the touchline, I looked across to the Jack Carr Stand, already busy with exuberant teenage Sandgrounders. One patted rhythms on a drum that conducted the others into particular songs. This, increasingly, was how younger supporters made their noise, from the very top of the game to Kendal, Workington and Southport. It was far closer to the orchestrated soundscape encountered in Italian or German stadiums, an internationalist approach for a worldly generation. Over time, crowd noise changes. The main thing is that it is there. Never had we known that truth more than in 2020.

They stood in twos or small groups making their noise, perhaps even over-compensating to verbally plug the physical gaps between them. Distancing rules were read once more over the tannoy, and a reminder to wear masks when tottering along to the tea bar too, before the impossibly perky *Grandstand* theme tune struck up.

The juxtaposition of grim Covid tidings with this evocative masterpiece that reminded me of simple childhood Saturdays simultaneously brought a lump to my throat and a tear to my eye. I made a noise somewhere between a laugh and a sigh. In a film, the woman next to me would have offered me consoling words and a tissue. We may even have one day married. Instead, she ushered her son to a different part of the stand, away from this disturbing bearded lunatic who apparently had a nervous tic that sounded like an asthmatic goose.

As the *Grandstand* theme reached a guitar solo I did not know it had – I pictured Des Lynam going full pelt on a Fender Stratocaster – the teams were read out in a suitably sprightly voice. 'And now for the mighty yellows that are Southport…' As in every ground since player names were first called, some were cheered more enthusiastically than others, and there came the usual tailing off for upper numbers and substitutes. Supporters have eight or nine fulsome salutes in them, then it becomes a bit like the part at a gig where a band announces: 'This is a new one we've been working on.'

'Please welcome the teams on to the pitch. Alfreton Town aaaaaaand Southport!' declared the breezy matchday ringmaster, injecting more seaside pizzazz. The drum gathered pace and the Jack Carr tifosi sang 'Yyyyyellows, yyyyyellows' and then a localised reinterpretation of 'Ring of Fire'. Their later repertoire would include versions of 'Can't Help Falling in Love' and 'Anarchy in the UK'. The terrace jukebox is an eclectic one.

The coin toss prompted a change of ends – an all too rare phenomenon – and in the seconds before kick-off I looked across to the main stand. There were three blocks of seating hosting supporters in duos or groups, then a middle block of club officials, and finally three blocks of lone spectators. Each person had been given a seat precisely apart from the next, and it gave the impression of a Lego stand and crowd created by an extremely precise child. It also seemed to emphasise that these fans were watching on their own in a ghetto of the lonesome.

The Sandgrounders wore shirts in the radioactive amber of Crunchy Nut Cornflakes, and Alfreton Town thin pink-and-blue stripes that brought to mind those fly-curtain door strips that so many houses used to have. Such flashy colours were in keeping with the seaside mood and could even have been inspired by the gaudy weave of an amusement arcade carpet. The game began and the players quickly worked their way through the usual phrasebook: 'Time, time', 'Man on!', 'Show for it' and all the rest.

Town slung the ball forward in search of striker Danny Clarke. He lowered his chin to his chest and hunted it down in the manner of an ostrich pursuing a mate. His bullish endeavours seemed for a while to turn the home defence into a collective nervous wreck. Each man looked as if he had heard the dreaded words 'Turn over your exam papers and begin'. It was no surprise when Alfreton's Nicky Walker broke their offside trap – more of a gentle decoy – and sprang clear. The Southport goalkeeper, Dan Hanford, repelled his effort. Soon afterwards, he lost patience with his defenders entirely, screaming, as a cross meandered in, 'I can't fucking well come for that!' He had become the huffy man at a pedestrian crossing who finally loses patience and reaches across others to push the button.

Southport lugged their way forward in retaliation. 'Have a dig, lads,' shouted a man near me, and they did – several efforts, in fact, each of which stoked a collective 'aaaawww' followed by rapid and encouraging applause, one of a football crowd's more pleasing sounds. For a while, the sides occupied the middle third of the pitch, each managing a few passes in succession before discarding the ball clumsily. It became a game of join the dots in which no pattern was ever properly completed.

It was during this period that Alfreton goalkeeper George Willis hooted the words 'Too much to do, TOO MUCH TO DO' at no one in particular. I thought about how all of these players were semi-professional and had jobs beyond football, and wondered if he was articulating anxiety over a particularly horrendous 'To Do' list from his regular job. We were also approaching Christmas, of course, a time of many demands.

The sun fell a notch or two and in late afternoon light Haig Avenue and those fairy-light kits on the pitch looked serenely beautiful. Once again, being at football felt like a wonderful privilege. Then Alfreton midfielder Bobby Johnson curled a shot into the Southport net and a man near me cried, 'Fuck's sake 'Port. I'm off for a Twix.'

Now Town began to tap the ball around and try to set Clarke free. His head-down style brought to mind a speedskater, his raised cubic shoulders a pub darts player. The creative influence attempting to prod chances from midfield was captain Dan Bradley. With his suede tan and bleached mane flapping like a grounded seagull in a state of panic, he looked to me like the flustered assistant manager of a Thomas Cook store.

Soon, the match found its shoddy rhythm again. Even the neat efforts of Bradley could not prevent a series of consecutive headers so protracted that supporters began to cheer each one. I have never really understood what constitutes such a figure, but any 'football purist' attending today was probably now standing at the end of Southport pier, staring into nothingness.

Southport entered the pitch for the second half a good few minutes before Alfreton. It was as if they had been sent out to try to discover the true meaning of football. The floodlights blinked into life, perhaps as a form of visual cue to the players in the manner of an ON AIR light in a radio studio.

Alfreton eventually joined them and the second half began. Songs soared from the Jack Carr Stand, with simpler numbers being echoed by supporters in every other part of the ground. After so long without football here – 269 days until last Wednesday's game with Farsley Celtic – scorelines did not matter as much as they used to, and even less so the spectacle on offer. It was an erroneous, atypical period, undoubtedly, but it scratched at the core of what supporting a team meant: being there, being home, however the team was doing. 'Allez allez allez oh,' they sang, 'Southport FC/yellow and black army.'

The noise faded for a while as it does from time to time across any game. I had the feeling that some around me were enjoying hearing the players again. 'Byline, stand on the byline.' 'Right shoulder, right shoulder.' 'Spin him, spin him.' These mantras of the turf were oddly mesmeric, and the decrees of the coaching staff teasingly intriguing, like cryptic crossword clues. 'You have to have a squeeze, you have to be brave,' shouted Alfreton manager Billy Heath at one point. 'Shut it, bald eagle,' replied a Southport fan.

Alfreton began to play a brisk type of football that pivoted around Johnson, a preening kind of midfielder. The home side responded directly and desperately, launching throw-ins towards the penalty area with all the accuracy of a toddler hurling a frisbee in a gale. Forward Marcus Carver made admirable attempts to win them all, but it was like watching a springer spaniel pursuing a fly.

As a special breed of terrace cold descended, in which whole contagious lines of toes enter a coma, the Sandgrounders perked up and began shooting from distance and shooting well. The referee issued corner kicks on repeat prescription. Yet nothing could beat Willis in the Town goal. Supporters began drifting towards exits, all resigned shrugs. Knowing statements of 'We'll not score if we play until midnight' were uttered to sons and daughters.

Then, in the 94th minute, they did. Departing fans turned on their heels and ran towards the elated cacophony like healed lepers. Substitute Jordan McFarlane-Archer had stabbed home an equaliser with the very last touch of the game. Canned for a minute were those weakling sentiments that just being here was joy enough: an injury-time leveller was sweet euphoric everything. On the Jack Carr terrace they pogoed like their dads used to. Right here, right now, football mattered more than it had since daffodils last bloomed.

The jolly ringmaster turned up Slade and said his farewells to 500 bouncing Sandgrounders: 'The next league match here is on Boxing Day when we host Curzon Ashton. So in that case, Happy Christmas, and please have a safe journey home.' They marched off homewards grinning, saluting and talking about the goal.

'We were the better side in the second half,' said a father to his sons. 'We murdered them.' 'Dad?' replied one of the boys. 'Can we get chips on the way home?'

'Course we can, lad,' replied his dad.

Christmas lights flashed in gardens and life felt full of promise and wonder again.

6

Cowdenbeath 2 v 0 Brechin City
Scottish Professional League Division Two

We lived a December with the hallmarks of any other. Every after-noon until the solstice, street lamps awoke a few minutes earlier than they had on the previous day. The festive season occupied supermarket aisles and broadcast airwaves. Spotting Christmas trees in the windows of homes delivered the usual twinkling comfort. On a bus, I heard a woman list her seasonal chocolate likes and dislikes, including the magnificent words: 'Not Bounties, though. I can't stand that defecated coconut stuff.'

Yet Christmas 2020 felt like a shadow yuletide and a replica: recognisable and yet distorted. It was possible to imagine Santa Claus dressed in black, or donkeys instead of reindeer. There was a certain collective guilt at feeling too much festive cheer. So many had suffered. Furthermore, in the fortnight after my Southport trip, a new term had been added to the country's Covid vernac-ular of clapping for carers, extended households, the Rule of Six et al: 'Variant'.

A mutated version of the original coronavirus, named the Alpha variant, was now among us. Rules and restrictions were tightened, although there would be special dispensation for people to spend Christmas together, a kind of jittery shore leave.

Remarkably, stunningly quickly, a vaccination programme had begun. Another lockdown, though, began to feel as unavoidable as a discount sofa advert on Boxing Day television.

One of football's entries in that patois of the pandemic was 'Behind Closed Doors'. The phrase had been used sparingly in the past to denote matches being played with no fans present, usually as a punishment from UEFA or FIFA. Now, it was the game's default mode, three words encapsulating an era. When they were spoken, a sad resignation that quietly singed with frustration and a famished sense of absence could be detected. Increasingly, it became clear that limited-crowd fixtures such as the one I'd attended at Haig Avenue were an exception. They were to be an aborted experiment rather than the first stirrings of supporters' eventual full return. Behind Closed Doors games would remain the dominant strain.

In Scotland, that had largely been the case at every level of football since it restarted after the March vanishing. There had been no concessions to the non-league or amateur game, and only a few limited-attendance trial matches. The Highland League postponed the start of its season until 28 November, when finally clubs in some areas were allowed 300 spectators owing to low Covid case numbers in the north of the country. At Rothes and Wick, they finally had their sainted, yearned-for return.

That same day, I'd attended a game in the Scottish Borders between Gala Fairydean Rovers and Kelty Hearts. Although I had wanted my stories from this secretive season to come from the terraces, reality – with its omnipresent closed doors – had finally guided me to the press box.

Galashiels, a mill town where spinning has long ceased, reclines in a lush valley. This serene situation has helped to infuse locals with a calm disposition and gentle humour. Before the game, a club official had caught me fixating on a wood pigeon attempting to peck food from the 3G pitch. 'Oh, that's Jim,' she said. 'We let him out before the teams come on. He's our version of the Benfica eagle.'

The location and architecture of Fairydean Rovers' stadium, Netherdale, is a frequent diversion from games. Look beyond one touchline and you may lose yourself in trees and hills. On the other side, the ground's unique main stand hooks attention. It is a brutalist, Category A-listed masterpiece. Perusing its angles and crevices, and wondering how on earth its roof remains upright, is an escapist distraction, like becoming engrossed in an old map. Though brutalism is not universally admired in the wider world, there is an almost universal affection for this stand in Scottish football. That afternoon's referee, John McKendrick, was adjudicating his very last game after a long career spent at the top of the sport. He had requested a fixture here for his retirement bow so that he could fulfil an ambition to referee beneath its magnificence.

On that ashen-skied afternoon, Netherdale offered a third enjoyable disruption to watching the match. He arrived at ten to three. The clatter of metal on wood jolted us and made us look towards the noise. First, we saw the two prongs of a ladder, poking up over the perimeter fence they were rested upon on the outside of the ground. Then, a head slowly emerged – fuzzy grey hair, followed by thick-rimmed spectacles and a chin that now rested on the barricade.

This floating apparition was a man in his sixties. Apparently, he had already watched a number of shut-out games propped up on his ladder. His actions showed an admirable determination not to be kept apart from his team; they were his love on the other side of a Berlin Wall. In a wonderfully mysterious twist, despite this being a homely club in a small town, no one seemed to know his identity. 'There was a rumour that he lives in the old folks' home on the hill,' said one club volunteer to me, 'but that's turned out to be a myth.' As the two captains jogged forward to toss a coin, he put on a beanie hat and a pair of chunky ski gloves, a belated disguise perhaps.

There was, however, nothing furtive about his demeanour through the rest of the game. Soon, he had risen three or four rungs and rested now above the fence, his arms balanced on its top beams. His support was ebulliently vocal too – 'Come on Gala!' and 'Ach away, referee' came the rasping cries. This defiance deserved more than a home defeat. Ladder Man had seen through closed doors.

* * *

Six days before our hollow Christmas, I took a train from Edinburgh to Fife. The sun hung low and dappled through the crimson beams of the Forth Rail Bridge. Down below in the dockyards of Rosyth, half a dozen cruise liners rested still, flashy white beasts with their casinos and golf strips mothballed by Covid. A Scotsman tried to explain the concept of Deep Sea World, an attraction beneath us in North Queensferry, to a young South American woman. 'So… there are fishes and you just look at them and then go home?' she said. I had the feeling she hoped it was more like one of those restaurants where guests choose which lobster they wish to eat.

As the train cantered into Fife, a woman broke off her phone call to choke mightily, and then resumed. 'So I says to the doctor,' she continued, 'it's a phlegmy cough, not a Covid cough.' It was the contemporary equivalent of rain souring a barbecue. I was not alone in moving to another carriage.

To look out of the window in west and central Fife now is to glance upon deep countryside and pendulous hills. Once, smoke, winding gear, pitheads and great thudding shipyards lined the way. Now, greenery has encroached on every annihilated industrial surface; many of those hills are old coal bings, resurfaced by nature. This was – *is*, to an extent – a hard place. Poetic local team names such as Crossgates Primrose, Dundonald Bluebell and Lochgelly Albert suggest romance was reserved for this county's national pastime: football.

From the centre of Cowdenbeath High Street, it is possible to see that the town is sinking. A coal mine is burrowed underneath, with the result that it sags visibly at its centre. This place is a pit town without the work a pit brings, but with the physical and emotional scars mining closures left behind. Regardless, it plods on resiliently. Gable-end murals and landscape gardening have smartened one area, and that afternoon blinking Christmas lights added hope. Yet nothing could disguise the amount of empty retail units strafing that undulating main artery. Even Greggs had closed down. Cowdenbeath struggled enough before Covid; its arrival twisted the knife.

In Poundstretcher – alongside B&M, the main supplier of matchday sweets during my pandemic season – two girls not much older than my ten-year-old daughter considered the shop's stationery offering. I reflected warmly on how soon it would be my girl's turn to spend Saturday mornings in town messing about with her friends, a fine tradition. 'No scented pens?' said one of the youngsters. 'What a fucking shambles of a shop.'

A Saltire rested limp over the town hall. For many years through the 20th century, they had flown the red flag here on the birthday of the Russian Revolution. Like so many mining places the world over, in Cowdenbeath abject underground conditions bred a togetherness that resulted in overground political solidarity. This was a radical town.

Almost a century ago, in April 1921, governing authorities were anxious. There was a suspicion that revolution was fomenting in this part of Fife. Soon, it could swell outwards and infect Glasgow, and then beyond. Amid press rumours of 'extremist plots' surrounding a miners' strike and rally, the British military occupied the town. A form of martial law was established. Locals 'woke up', reported the *Dunfermline Press*, 'to find that the burgh had been converted into what was virtually an armed camp.' Arrested miners sang 'The Red Flag' as they were escorted to the cells.

That action was broken, but Fife miners retained their radicalism for over half a century. As late as 1973, there were a dozen communist councillors covering Cowdenbeath and its surrounding areas. A year on, former miner Willie Sharp became Britain's first communist provost (mayor). There is little now that sings of this past, although a 15-minute walk uphill can still land you at a street named for a great Soviet hero of yesterday's Fife: Gagarin Way. The long strike of 1984 was both a climax of these convictions and the beginning of their dwindling.

By the Sunshine on Beath café, I set off for Central Park, Cowdenbeath FC's incomparable home ground. High on a pebble-dashed wall, a concise next-game board trumpeted today's fixture against Brechin City. That the board had been updated felt mildly impressive; given that no local could attend, there was essentially no product to advertise. Such things could easily have been left to decay in these demoralising times. Low in the chain, football clubs run on local pride.

Both Cowdenbeath and Brechin were playing out seasons of woe and misfortune. The home side occupied the penultimate spot in Scottish League football, their visitors the last. Victory for the latter today would see a reversal of that sorry order, one bedevilled drunk stumbling over the paralytic and prone body of another.

Central Park has long been a dual venue. The football club's need to raise money has made it a ground with a split personality: noosing the turf is a track that greyhounds and various vehicles have darted around through the years. Signs welcome both football visitors and those to Cowdenbeath Racewall: The Home of Scottish Stock Car Racing. On many Saturday matchdays, goalposts are removed and engines snarl before the teams have even left the pitch. In the final minutes of games, it is possible to imagine stock-car drivers at the sidelines, twirling and twiddling their car keys in the manner of impatient dads at pick-up time.

This financial necessity arose after the club's finest period, from the mid-1920s to 1930s. Back then, miners used their spare coins to watch a team of their own – men who worked Saturday mornings in the pit and Saturday afternoons on the pitch. No man could truly forget his toil – winding gear loomed over the main stand – but in regularly snaring Celtic, Rangers and other leading lights, Cowdenbeath offered escapism and stardust. The Hungry

Thirties, however, left pockets and terraces empty. Sometimes it feels as though the club has struggled through every day since.

* * *

In a repurposed turnstile block, fluorescent volunteers took the temperatures of media guests and club officials, we few blessed souls permitted to watch. Earlier in the week, Scottish supporters had once again climbed stepladders to see a game, this time at Deveronvale FC's Princess Royal Park. Others had peeped through single fence knotholes like so many Cyclops in red and white scarves. I recalled that earlier in the season, Aberdeen fans had ascended over their Pittodrie Stadium in a cherry picker to watch a fixture with Rangers. Such is the distance between the public road and Central Park's stands, similar efforts would have required a whole new level of subterfuge involving binoculars and a crane.

In these spaces lingered clutter and debris. These corroding remnants made this ground unrivalled in its uniqueness. Behind one entrance gate sat an old tractor. Then came giant tyres and indeterminate agricultural equipment. They added a certain junkyard ambience, the footballing equivalent of meandering around an antiques showroom. 'It's Your Cowdenbeath Thursday Open Market' declared a vintage sign above one doorway, only adding to the air of *Bargain Hunt* on acid.

'The press box is in the old bit,' said an amiable steward. He signalled towards the furthest of two main stands, split close to the halfway line and by the decades. This stunted earlier enclosure is an old work of wooden benches and iron beams. In the early 1990s, fire ravaged the complete building and left a cavity, which was then filled by a steel and concrete replacement. It gives the impression of a home being shared out of financial necessity by a divorced couple with very different tastes.

Despite the stark melancholia of a matchday without fans, there were faint impressions of this game's quarter-to-three cabaret. Perhaps old places like this just cannot help it, as if this magic hour is a clockwork occurrence or it seeps from the walls.

It helped that a homespun cast had begun to appear – committee men in suits and their manicured wives greeted one another, club types in their crested puffa jackets inspected teamsheets and journalists tip-tapped through fingerless gloves.

Down on the pitch, furthering this impression of more pleasingly humdrum times, squat generals in polyester made younger men run around cones, and by the dugouts the match officials huddled from a rain shower like pensioners in a bus shelter. Eventually, they found the courage to begin their warm-up, trotting reluctantly over the turf in the fashion of cats on snow. With this encounter taking place so close to the shortest day of the year, the Central Park floodlights were already casting their radiant sheen. Meanwhile, the amber lamps of the old stand bathed us in the haze of a fridge light.

Players, coaches and officials left the field and tannoy music cut as suddenly and cleanly dead as at 2am in a nightclub. A fog of contemplative silence set in. Too many of us could hear our own thoughts. It was broken by a sound wholly unexpected in a lower division Scottish football ground: a deep and resonant Texan accent. 'God brought me to Brechin,' said the American, 'I'm a minister there.' He was, too, the man charged with filming highlights of City's games, this season a task of faith and sacrifice.

Though I would have liked to ask him for a view on the home side's entrance music – 'Livin' on a Prayer' by Bon Jovi – he seemed too entangled in questions of team line-ups. 'Which Iain Russell is that?' he called across. 'The Iain Russell with two Is?' I shrugged my shoulders. I had not computed what he meant and wondered if there was another footballer by that name with only one – or perhaps three – eyes.

Players jogged on the spot to chase away the falling cold and referee Barry Cook counted them, a scout leader at the camping-trip minibus door. Some of them seemed to look distractedly over to Central Park's ample terracing. They resembled lonely sailors whom nobody had turned up to wave off. Or perhaps, in this crowd-free landscape, some of them saw apparitions in bobble hats or noticed the Burger Meats Chips snack bar for the first time.

'Livin' on a Prayer' died back as it must, and the geeing-up warbles of footballers and their benches could be heard. 'Let's boss this' came the cry from a Brechin tracksuit. 'Intae their faces, Cowden' responded a home figure.

Eccentrically for a team nagged by relegation anxiety, Cowden attacked from defence. Right-back Fraser Mullen pecked away at the flanks, his blond hair bobbing like tumbleweed on a beach. Colossal centre-half Jamie Todd, whose sleeves reached only to his upper arms in the style of a spinach-bingeing Popeye, pushed the ball into midfield and lolloped after it. His defensive partner, the captain Craig Barr, scampered out of defence with elegance, always finding a forward-bound teammate.

Attempting to halt these bombastic surges was a task that fell for the most part to the City midfielder Michael Paton. That the neat and able Paton was also player-manager and captain wrought a heavy burden on him. By five o'clock, he wore the jaded look of a man sentenced to never again know why he had walked into a particular room Every one of his jobs must have felt like trying to unwrap a Chupa Chups lollipop while wearing oven gloves.

Though it lacked a tangible chorus, the game soon fell into a rhythm of sorts, namely two teams frenetically pushing forward before spooning the ball straight to the opposition goalkeeper. Both sides had a fantastic hunger but no teeth. This pattern was embodied in two early moments. First, Kris Renton – a gifted player with shoulders like loaves of bread that could feed the five thousand – attempted to kill the ball dead in preparation for a shot. Instead, he succeeded only in letting it run wildly through his legs. With no supporters present, this mishap barely registered, as if such moments require sarcastic jeers to truly count – 'If a tree falls in the woods…?' Then, City's Connor Coupe notched the game's first shot on target. Coupe struck the ball from outside the box but it seemed to lose pace with every inch it travelled, a clay pigeon that had changed its mind and wanted to go home. The effort travelled so far down goalkeeper Ross Munro's throat that it seemed like the Heimlich manoeuvre might be required to remove it.

Then, a platoon of the Cowdenbeath defence snapped once more into action. Mullen sprinted forward to take a corner with the frantic energy of a man running home to check he'd not left the immersion heater on. He then looped the kick enticingly into the box. There waited the leaping Barr, who seemed to convince the ball into the net with his head. Teammates bolted over to celebrate. Their uproar of elation could be clearly and refreshingly heard; such an outpouring of hedonism had been a rare thing indeed in doleful and meek 2020. When the noise relented, the Brechin right-back, Ewan McLevy, looked over to the bench and shouted 'Fucking pish', a comment far more of its epoch.

His team rose from the canvas. In one attack, Cowden's Todd seemed to steam-press spiky City forward Martin Scott to the floor. No penalty was given. Scott's neck tattoos appeared to spin and swirl in anger. The Central Park hush allowed his colleagues' yelps of appeal to be heard. Their falsetto remonstrations brought to mind the shrieks of seagulls fighting over discarded chips.

This rumpus seemed to usher forth a period of empty, contemplative silence punctured solely by the referee's whistle. It was as if he was the only man allowed to talk through silent prayer. That man Todd bashed a long-range strike extravagantly over the bar and on to the vacant terraces. 'Christ's sake, Jamie,' called someone from the home bench. If nothing else, it roused those of us in the stands and diverted our thoughts from the sheer futility of existence. Then, a freight train heaved by on the track that runs close to Central Park, and keeper Munro rapped his studs against a goalpost. Both sounds were, in their own way, industrial reminiscences – one recalled coal wagons on the move, the other made a noise not unlike steel rivets being thrashed into place. Neither deep silences nor incidental hubbub, nor champion dugout swearing, would have been detected with fans in the ground; a different – albeit unwanted – layer of intrigue had been added.

The referee's half-time whistle pierced the air like the call of some exotic bird announcing it had completed this winter's nest. Back drifted substitutes from their warm-up spots by the race-track traffic lights, and back came the starting players over the chequered patches of the stock car finishing line.

At half-time it was possible to fixate mostly on what we didn't hear: no lotto numbers or birthday wishes, and scores from other grounds announced without cheers or sneers of fan reaction. Footballs were re-sanitised and deposited in their resting places at intervals alongside the pitch, and the second half began. 'Come on Brechin,' howled the Texan, with the lustre and weight of the true believer. I sat hoping his speech was about to evolve into an evangelical gospel number about the relegation dogfight.

In the hard winter dark, Brechin stirred. They were cajoled onwards by Paton, who had possibly shouted at himself in the dressing-room mirror. Still Barr repelled everything, either striding out of defence with the ball intact or entering into aerial challenges like a man hurtling towards Earth in a faulty parachute. Perhaps convinced he was unbeatable, City began to look crestfallen. Soon, Iain 'two eyes' Russell scored a second goal, finishing with cunning after the ball had spun madly in the manner of an escaped Catherine wheel. Cowdenbeath players piled on top of one another in a clumsy pyre and again their salutes momentarily argued back against 2020.

Now they began to play a different sport and belong to another part of the league table, as if the earlier portion of the season had been a fancy-dress act. Renton, despite running in the vexed manner of a father late for his child's nativity play, was a revelation of pirouettes and flicks. There were long sequences of snappy, slick passing. Where the breeze could, a year ago, have carried accompanying cries of 'Olé', now it wafted over only the eerie chimes of 'Greensleeves' from a nearby ice-cream van. When finally his team received possession, a Brechin defender discharged a long ball so wayward that I wondered whether he was attempting to grenade the van's speaker. Most of his team looked as if they were about to start crying or hit one another, the archetypal family at Christmas.

The last whistle sounded, Brechin were marooned at the table's foot and the Texan looked to the blank sooty sky. 'What can you do?' he asked in resignation. Cowdenbeath were applauded from the field by those few allowed to be here. Shorn of its devotees, Central Park had been no empty vessel, nor a soulless void. Its seasoned walls saw to that, as did the rich emotion coursing through the team that afternoon. Yet being there without fans was like sitting in the beloved armchair of a now departed grandparent.

Beneath the floodlit gleam outside, it was possible to imagine silhouettes bobbing gently into the cold night with talk of away-day plans and thoughts of league tables – the ghosts of people that were alive and well, just forbidden from going home.

On the journey home I tried to concentrate on football results but found cloying reality hard to escape. Politicians once more leaned on their podiums and looked into camera lenses. The Covid variant was rampaging. Christmas shore leave was cancelled. Already, January in the United Kingdom sounded like an even bleaker proposition than usual.

* * *

In that bloated purgatory between Christmas and New Year, I was commissioned by a German football magazine to write a profile of the Rangers manager, Steven Gerrard. Press access for the Old Firm derby match on 2 January was impossible at short notice. I would witness this usually rambunctious and frequently toxic fixture from the closed gates of Rangers' Ibrox Stadium. Somehow, this necessity felt apt.

Glasgow that morning seemed to radiate with stillness. Traffic lights changed for invisible pedestrians and magpies window-shopped. A cloudless blue sky added to the serenity, its pale sun shrouding delicious light on the city's red-and-blond sandstone buildings. Police loitered outside Ibrox underground station. They stared intently at the subway exit as if they saw ghost legions of football fans walking towards the stadium and kick-off. The build-up to a traditional New Year Old Firm fixture had never been so tranquil. Everyone hoped it never would be again. That game, that city, needed its noise.

Ibrox Stadium looms among rows of tenement housing in the old shipbuilding district of Govan. It is a colossus dropped among the everyday urban. To experience it stagnant on derby day felt like a strange dream. Three of its stands are plain, though each is adorned with images of great Gers players of yesteryear. Every football ground needs its fairy tales. The exception is Ibrox's red-brick main stand, a work of monumental beauty by the great Glaswegian stadium architect, Archibald Leitch. Although Leitch designed stands at more than 20 British grounds from Anfield to White Hart Lane, this is the finest of his works. With its long, thin windows and stone flourishes, it resembles some kind of industrial church.

Even with the Ibrox turnstiles shuttered, standing outside it was again possible to observe some characteristics of a normal matchday. There was still a stench of manure left by police horses. The stadium's PA system boomed ferociously, and the main stand reception area bustled as usual with players, officials and various lanyard men arriving. Sadly, representing the cancer that infests this fixture, a group of bigots had appeared and howled anti-Catholic abuse at the Celtic team as they climbed from their bus and entered the stadium. It was one element of a regular Old Firm day that not many of us missed.

Nothing, though, could disguise how macabre this Covid-era matchday was. Outside a stadium of 50,000 people, it should be impossible to comprehend the referee's whistle and the bellowing of coaches and players. Everything was audible from the street. It was as if we could suddenly hear underwater.

At two corners of Ibrox are grand iron gates proclaiming 'Rangers Football Club Ltd'. Half a dozen football refugees gathered by one of them. I talked first to John, a disabled man of 64 years old who moved around in a wheelchair. Smiling with his face pressed to the iron gates, he resembled a prisoner dreaming of life on the outside, of freedom. In a way he was. Through a gap, John could see a small portion of the pitch and, if he squinted hard enough, half of the goal at the other end. Every now and then, the match action drifted into his segment and he barked encouragement at a Rangers player or mocked a rival. He did not even have a radio: 'The rest of it I try to get from listening to the players. Or I just guess.' John told me that he had been attending Rangers matches since 1956.

A teenage boy cycled up and found his own slither of pitch to study. He stared, enchanted, a child watching Father Christmas through a crack in the living-room door. 'I think it's a penalty!' he exclaimed after voices heightened on the pitch. He told me that he had never been inside the stadium, even before Covid struck. 'I don't have the money. So, I've never seen them in real life. But I will one day.'

There was an even younger supporter than him at the gate – a couple had brought their four-month-old son for 'His first Old Firm. He's come to see us win the title.' This, then, was the main cast of gate refugees, while others drifted by and later left as the game progressed.

All the time, stewards circled nearby and police officers sat in warm vans, looking on curiously as this bunch of strangers craned their necks to see a few metres of action. Some people will do anything to be near football. Rangers scored and those gathered congratulated each other and slapped their hands against the iron prongs that kept them from their team.

Around the corner were flowers. The second of January is a date circled in black on the Glasgow calendar. Today, it was precisely 50 years since the Ibrox Disaster. On 2 January 1971, 66 supporters were crushed to death at Stairway 13 while leaving the Old Firm fixture. Someone, it is thought, fell down, causing another person to fall on top of him and then creating a devastating domino effect. Iron railings buckled under the weight of bodies. Half of those who died were under 20 years old. Five friends from the small Fife town of Markinch perished, their ages between 13 and 15.

There were hundreds of flower bouquets spread around Ibrox that afternoon, some next to the official memorial, and some left in turnstile entrances and other places of individual, unspoken significance. The first flower card I read was dedicated to Nigel Pickup, at eight years old the tragedy's youngest victim. 'Taken far too soon' and 'We cherish the short memories we have', it said. By grim coincidence, like Steven Gerrard, Nigel was a Liverpudlian. He was visiting Glasgow for New Year. The second of January 1971 was his first, and last, match. There are, too, flowers from the Hillsborough Ibrox Memorial Group. This most grievous of bonds was one Gerrard knew well. At ten years old, a cousin of his, Jon-Paul Gilhooley, was the youngest victim of the Hillsborough disaster.

Back by the iron gate, I asked John what he remembered of that dreadful afternoon half a century ago. He confirmed that he had attended the match but did not want to say much more, beyond mentioning a terrible injury suffered by his sister on Stairway 13. This, like Hillsborough, is a tragedy still being lived, not some event from another, more barbaric age.

The final whistle sounded and the refugees clapped and cheered. They had a victory, and a 19-point lead at the top of the table, some fuel for optimism in a jaded world. John did not merely look like he was about to walk again for the first time in years, he looked like he was about to fly. A passing taxi driver hooted his car horn several times as if we were in Sicily and not Scotland, and fireworks were released into the daylight sky. Ecstatic sounds tumbled from the windows of impounded Govan. It was, by pandemic era standards, a delightful scene.

A few minutes later, back at the underground station, it was as if nothing had happened. 2021 had begun, and streets and stadiums had emptied all over again.

7

30/01/21
Raith Rovers 3 v 1 Dundee
Scottish Professional League Championship

It seemed to be the longest January in history. A whole month in which every minute crawled along like a classroom clock during double maths. Comfort was scarce, although decipherable in the unblinking cycle of nature; birds snatched twigs for their nests, snowdrops still nudged through and snow itself appeared and made everywhere timeless. Lockdown had fallen around us too, and would still be here beyond daffodils and lambs.

Our Covid language now included talk of 'mutant strains', variations of the disease far worse than those we had known. All the wrong numbers continued to rise. Many more people who were loved passed away and became numbers on the news. Robotic condolences were offered by politicians. The vaccination programme signalled that life could one day be rosy again, and yet January 2021 was the bleakest spell of the pandemic so far. Again, we had our personal stresses beyond the societal – home-schooling children, missing faraway relatives, being unable to visit elderly parents – but this time chill winds blew and it felt like a film with no end.

Some argued that football should once more be halted, or at least did not understand why it had the privilege of continuing when so many other sports, pastimes and cultural pursuits were again abandoned. Those, though, were decisions above the mere supporters. They were left to feel grateful for whatever television game or online feed could be found. Some had managed to attend matches during that late summer-to-autumn sweet spot, or during the brief December reprieve. Many had not been inside a ground for almost a year. All agreed that this would only ever be half a sport while supporters were locked out. There was a feeling, too, that even in its emaciated, behind-closed-doors state, watching one's team, or even just *knowing* they were playing, offered great mental relief – and occasionally joy – for those of us under football's spell.

Followers of some clubs did not even have screen privileges. Much of England's non-league, including all of the levels I had watched fixtures at so far, had been suspended. In Scotland, the bottom two SPFL divisions and the non-league game hung in the same purgatory. The concept of supporters being allowed back into grounds had been almost entirely wiped from the agenda. Now, we shrugged our shoulders, as with all the annulled plans, cancelled holidays and refund policies we had experienced over the past ten months. It did not stop us closing our eyes and projecting ourselves on to bustling terraces, though. Nor could we halt slow salty tears when a piece of music or a smell took us back there.

As January slowly rotted away, I returned to Fife. Kirkcaldy is a post-industrial town on the coast, although many of its buildings face away from the water as if trying to avoid eye contact. Today, that elephant-coloured water – the Firth of Forth – rumbled away before arriving against the Esplanade wall in something of a tirade. Two container ships lay still, waiting for a cloud to blubber on them. A dozen or so people had gathered, back in the dreaded monotony of their daily lockdown walks, and looked out in their direction. 'Ach, and you think we moan about being lonely,' said one old lady to another. 'Imagine being on one of those.'

There was a profound, if familiar, loneliness to the high street too. The silver shutters of closed shops reflected on the flagstones of soggy pavements. At the end nearest the sea, no person walked by despite the enticingly rare lights and open doors of a minimart named 'Touch of Poland and Other Countries'. Close by, a pedestrian crossing beeped but no red or green men appeared, as if they too had stayed at home.

There was more life to be found further on. In the doorway of a barren former BHS store, a busker wearing the scraggly grey hair and rumpled beard of Karl Marx sang beautifully, first 'Wonderwall' and then 'Sunshine on Leith'. An old man made a short and jolly jinking manoeuvre, then winked at the busker and put a few coins by his dog. In such moments, beneath the glummest of skies in the drabbest of times, did it feel like things could and would get better. There was even laughter outside Specsavers, where a man had spotted the growing queue, joined and asked: 'Is this a nightclub?' Still, how we longed for shops deemed non-essential to open once more. Then, for a day when no outlet would need signs limiting themselves to two or three 'Households' at any one time, another of those words seldom heard before spring 2020, or distance markings on the floor.

Walking through streets of handsome villas at the top of the town, I rounded a corner and was summoned by floodlights. They poked out above a row of terraced houses like the ears of a wolf sneaking up on a rodent. Raith Rovers' Stark's Park is exactly where a football ground should be: just out of the town centre, among the homes of its people. The parish church. With that congregation housebound, no one queued outside Bobby's Snack Bar for a foam tray of sallow chips and no child begged for sweets from The Wee Shop on The Corner. Their scarves went unworn. Clouds tried to make amends by forming stripes with the sky, but it was not yet late enough in the day for Rovers' deep blue.

* * *

Stark's Park loafs on the ridge of a hill. This position swells the ground's frame and stature, as if the edges of its stands have been underlined in ink. After the stand behind one goal, there is nothing but a drop. Detracting from its dramatic posture as if slapping it across the cheek, Pratt Street leans in, meaning that Rovers have only ever had a curtailed nub of a main stand. A fine consequence of this is that those approaching can snoop happily inside, as if a cross-section has been removed for their benefit in the manner of a children's 'How Things Work' book. This is a tantalising offer for any supporter: *soon I'll be in there*. Catching a glimpse inside the stadium is a promise, one of the great moments of matchday anticipation.

That abridged main stand – almost a century old – begins close to the halfway line and unrolls in an L-shape to a point beyond a corner flag. Down beneath, where Pratt Street descends, chiselled into a wall are bricked-up turnstile entrances, probably contemporaries of the stand itself. One is at least twice as narrow as the other – the children's gate, perhaps. In the signs above them, so many layers of paint have overruled each other that it is only possible to make out one word: 'Grandstand', now departed from the language of the game with 'dubbin' and 'half-back'. Such heritage, ghost features of a ground are always affecting; given the barricades raised against fans attending today, even more so.

The stand's interior is similarly evocative. From my press box seat with its green tick safety sticker, it was possible to marvel at this example of what football stands were with an unhindered view. Being alone in the museum allowed time and space to observe birds nesting among its lattice of joists, beams and rafters. It meant noticing the ornate curves of the ironwork supporting row after row of wooden seats, which looked like gartered can-can legs poised for dancing. And it granted the regal surroundings that my increasingly enjoyable pursuit of watching Scottish match officials warm up deserved. This time, I fixed upon a nonchalant assistant referee with the running style of a teenager pretending to hurry up. It occurred to me that it must be odd for a linesman to suddenly have to run forwards rather than sideways, perhaps like asking a crab to stick to his lane.

At 3pm, a shard of dim sunlight pierced the Pratt Street chasm. It painted a broad sash of the artificial turf in kitchen sponge-scourer green. A litter of Dundee substitutes and squad members arrived and occupied a block of seats across the gangway from the press box. Some greeted ex-teammates who now played for Raith as they filed by to their own billets – 'Speak to ye efter, big man' and 'Guid tae see ye, pal'. I forget too easily that being a footballer is a job, and that the players that so many of us hang our happiest times and hopes upon have ex-colleagues that they miss (or not), tea rounds and Secret Santa draws. A middle-aged woman in a Dundee FC bench coat reminded them all to wear their face masks. Each young man obeyed in a way they never would have had a referee made the request. All mums must be heeded.

After five minutes, all of them stood to cheer, a replacement crowd. Their team had scored. The goal was plundered by Osman Sow, a Swede, but part manufactured by a Dundonian once of Liverpool but now playing a career encore with his beloved boyhood team: Charlie Adam.

At just over six feet tall, shaven-headed and with the impregnable torso of a hard-drinking lifeboatman, Adam is a rugged virtuoso. From the moment he jogged on to the pitch with a raised chin and chest in the style of some snuffed-up Edwardian sporting all-rounder, I revelled in watching him. There is such pleasure in observing a craftsman at work, whether sporting or otherwise, and wherever you are.

For much of the game, Adam occupied the middle third of the pitch. He sprinted rarely and only jogged when necessary, and yet controlled whole parchments of play, a scriptwriter sitting calmly feeding lines from centre stage. There was a noticeable difference in the rudiments of the game where this midfielder was concerned: he seemed to kick the football *differently*, approaching it with his left foot from an alternate, slighter and more tender angle. It was almost side-on, a kind of raking or a sweep of calligraphy. He did not just deal in delicacy; that method could be reinforced with concrete, so that long crossfield passes artfully but speedily found their way home and made previously aloof full-backs twitch and panic. There was sadness that so many thousands of people had so far missed seeing his homecoming exhibition, but selfish bliss in being able to obsess in near silence.

Midway through the first half, Adam carefully walloped a long pass with such clout that the ball seemed to visibly cower. Almost instantly, the floodlights came on, perhaps rudely awoken. This in sequence roused the Rovers' attack, as if they were werewolves unleashed by moons in four corners. The pack won a corner. In the penalty area, markers and marked jostled and twisted in a straight line, the performers of a feral ceilidh dance. When the ball hovered in, home centre-half Kyle Benedictus made a short curving jump that turned his body into a parenthesis and headed in an equaliser.

There was, once again, satisfaction in hearing the raptures of footballers, and knowing in that instant that they cared every bit as much as those pumping their fists in front of computer screens at home. That welcome noise faded rapidly. With no follow-up songs tumbling from the stands and no roar for the scorer's name, inside a minute a crow decluttering his wings while perched on a beam was the only noise the terraces could summon.

Rovers urged themselves onwards. They had calculated now the importance of keeping the ball from Adam, treating him as a piggy in the middle. Timmy Abraham, a debutant Fulham loanee, rasped in a shot that rolled first along the surface and began to rise, an aeroplane at take-off. The Dundee goalkeeper, Jack Hamilton, interrupted its flight, catching the ball stock-still with the snap of a mousetrap seizing its prey. His team seemed perturbed by Rovers' progression. Nineteen-year-old central defender Sam Fisher calmly escorted the ball out of defence, rolled his foot over it while contemplating his options, and then banjaxed a 20-yard pass straight to Rovers' manager John McGlynn in the home dugout. It was very possibly the footballing equivalent of a schoolboy raising his hand and calling the teacher 'Mum'.

Towards half-time, Adam's intense courtship with the ball was rekindled. His foot whispered and it responded, arcing around opponents or twirling suddenly. With the whistle near, he made a rare dart forward, pursuing one of his own ranging passes in the manner of someone chasing a pickpocket through a busy street. He gave up halfway. That facet of the sport was not for a man of 35. For every footballer, it must be unsettling to reach a fourth decade and become aware of their diminishing selves. It is hard to think of any profession beyond sport in which professionals have an inbuilt obsolescence that begins to show in their late twenties. At least Adam would always have his magic feet. In 50 years, he will be bending satsumas around the communal television of his old people's home.

Beginning the second period, Rovers rolled the ball to striker Lewis Vaughan. From a position just inside his own half, he surged forward. His actions seemed to recreate those Sunday morning players who try to dribble around every opponent straight from kick-off. As happens so often with them, Vaughan was thwarted before he departed the centre circle. Not that it would perturb this indefatigable soul, who had in the past returned from three separate anterior cruciate ligament injuries of the type that have frequently ended careers. On every field are yarns in the tapestry.

Ten minutes later, Dundee hooked the ball clear after a corner. As it spun in the air, Rovers' right-back Reghan Tumilty dashed towards it. He cushioned its flow, allowed it to bounce, paused as if asking it to dance and then potted it into the goal from 30 yards out. Having left his foot, it did not touch the floor again until the net catapulted it back over the line. Tumilty tore away in ecstasy. Maybe as he celebrated in front of the stands, he imagined a crowd as a child might in his garden.

His was a strike that embodied my feelings about the muzzled and disinfected model of football that I was being allowed to watch: on the one hand, moments like this, or smelling grass or watching floodlit shadows gave me a sense of giddy privilege; on the other, these places were hollow without their regulars, and these fixtures a form of spectral half-matches. I felt both *spoilt*, compared to those shut-out millions, and that I was spoil*ing* my own love of the game – perhaps I should have waited like everyone else. The devil hissed, 'That was a bloody good goal, though' and the angel lamented, 'Yes, but think of the poor souls who missed it.'

Back among the oak seats, a removed Dundee player – Paul McMullan – doddered his way to a perch, his chest still pumping. 'You'll need your coat, Paul. And a mask,' said mum. His replacement was Jason Cummings, a low-socked terrier who paced around energetically like a kid playing tig on his own. His presence seemed to startle the home side into action. A few minutes after Cummings' arrival, they scored again.

'Long way to go lads, a long way to go,' called over manager McGlynn as his team reset for kick-off. There was a slightly worried, forlorn air in his voice. There is much to admire about this avuncular Edinburgh man. High among his attributes, one of his former players told me, is how in team talks McGlynn would refer to the railway line that runs adjacent to Stark's Park and declare: 'Let's make sure we've scored by the time that 3.18 goes past.' In a game of analytical pomposity and Expected Goal metrics, this is a particularly charming notion.

His charges seemed to heed the warning. For much of the time that remained, they swarmed over their visitors. The away side frequently appeared static while Rovers ran around them. It was like a game of musical chairs in which only Dundee could hear when to stop. Adam toiled away, flighting the ball forward as if posing a question with it. He also became agitated and scrapped enough to warrant a booking. Cummings chased everything that sailed near him but with little profit. Near the end, he slung himself towards a cross but succeeded only in floating through the air. His arms and legs flailed, as if he were a pantomime villain being hoisted away on ropes. The life of a striker can be a lonely one.

Raith popped the ball around until finally ten to five came. With no applause to give or take, both teams swiftly dissolved from the pitch. Retracting wooden seats donked heavily in the main stand cavern and somebody shepherded the corner flags back to their cupboard. Whenever supporters were permitted to walk down Pratt Street and come home to Stark's Park, football would be ready for them. It was the same everywhere, only we had no notion of when that might be.

* * *

From an upstairs window in my house, I can see a football stadium. It is only a fragment of roof and a few ribcage beams painted in Subbuteo green, but it still counts. Open the window on a matchday in a regular season and the noises rising from that ground – Hibernian's Easter Road – can be heard. Here is my version of the little boy in *The Snowman* waking up, drawing the curtains and seeing his garden blanketed in white.

Often, I have eavesdropped only the build-up – tannoy cranking up, the testing of alarm tones, the furtive chants of early away fans – before departing at 2.45pm to attend the game, usually with my daughter. Living so close and leaving so late feels oddly old-fashioned, a throwback delight.

It had been 11 months since we last strolled hand in hand up the road to watch Hibs. In that time, we'd occasionally walked past the ground, always stopping and peeping through any gaps in the fence we could find, or even making a dedicated pilgrimage as a very loose part of home-schooling (History? Geography? Reading Ultras Stickers on Lamp Posts Studies?). The stadium began to feel like a relic from another time and a different way of life. Edinburgh had the castle and Leith had Easter Road.

At the start of the 2020/21 season, the footballers had come back. We could hear them. Opening our window allowed us to capture noises and interpret them as pictures: the referee's peeved whistle, the wailed penalty appeals. The fact that after-goal music was still played allowed for celebratory dancing. Hell, one week we even made macaroni pies.

Despite my thickening misgivings about attending behind-closed-doors matches, I felt the need to see inside. One week on from the Raith Rovers match, I would swap the blue lanyard for a green one and take in Hibs' Scottish Premier League game with Aberdeen. Leaving my daughter at the front door, our scarves and bobble hats on their hooks, made me feel like the kind of father who pops out for a packet of cigarettes and isn't seen again for 27 years.

Down comatose Hawkhill Avenue and on jilted Albion Place, takeaway trays eddied in the breeze and a pigeon floated in a small reservoir left by an overflowing drain. Earlier in the week, I had seen a fox investigating a discarded skateboard. It was a very inner-city version of nature's healing powers and urban rewilding. Perhaps it was Leith's answer to the mountain goats who had paraded through deserted Llandudno during lockdown, or those dolphins that had ventured further than ever before down the marine-traffic-free Bosphorus at the same time.

When I thought about other padlocked grounds, the soundtrack I missed was of programme and lotto callers. Here, in the usually bustling area by the club shop where supporters cross each other in a maelstrom while heading to their stands, I wanted to press Play and listen to Saturday acquaintances. It was in this spot that they gathered with their brief and friendly score predictions, and that old men told their granddaughters: 'Ach it's too cold to snow the day, doll.' The only hubbub came from those queuing for a Covid test in the community centre that shares the club car park.

From the press box, an eyrie high in the main stand, the warm-up shots of Hibs and Aberdeen players sounded like a distant firework display. You saw them being hit before you heard them. Beyond the gap between the stands opposite, a dab of the Firth of Forth could be seen, its water today a grizzly copper shade.

Easter Road is now a tight, equilateral kind of stadium. In its more charming – and raucous – days, its four sides had the differing heights of a family. Many other Edinburgh details and landmarks – mountains, hills, tenements, monuments – could be fixed upon and enjoyed during particularly dull games. There was much to be said for such higgledy-piggledy grounds that let the outside world in. They were, in a sense, more *of* their place, more connected instead of barricaded from their surroundings by a quartet of lanky bodyguards.

These neat and balanced places miss their characterful discrepancies, their gnawed parts and their scuffed edges. Yet, though Easter Road's modern hermetic enclosures have their muscular screen ends, how the wind still blows in and how it can, over the course of two hours, rap your neck like a whip and turn your ears into rigid seashells. Breeze blocks, steel and fibreglass can't halt the Edinburgh weather – it has a permanent season ticket here.

As was the way with all Covid-era fixtures, today's sides changed clothes in different parts of the ground prior to 90 minutes of intense, close physical contact. Aberdeen emerged from what was usually this ground's away end. In the same way that Covid has resulted in some societal changes that people prefer to the old ways – talking to neighbours, table service in pubs, not sharing a room with work colleagues – I wondered whether this alteration might enhance football once supporters returned. Reawakening the limp, choreographed spectacle that teams entering the pitch had become, each could enter from among their most vociferous followers like wrestlers or boxers. They might even crowd-surf on to the pitch. It would add a Roman Colosseum atmosphere sadly lacking from the modern game.

The teams took their starting positions and an alien noise kidnapped the airwaves. At first, it recalled the reverberating din made when a child blows raspberries and hums down a cardboard tube lined up against somebody else's ear. I wanted to say 'Stop that' and then grab the tube and do it back to the child, as I would have at home. Then it mutated into the scrunching noise made when a group of people walk over a vast gravel drive. Voices began, as if those people were talking to one another. And then I realised that they were singing.

Piped crowd noise was not a new phenomenon in Covid football. Ever since the commencement of televised games live from empty stadiums in June 2020, broadcasters had dabbled with fake hubbub, chanting, cheering and jeering. Some gave the option of watching matches with or without dubbed terraces. However, I had not considered that any club would attempt the same through its tannoy system. It felt immediately dystopian, the most darkly surreal moment in nigh on a year of them. It was disconcerting, disorientating and, frankly, weird. It seemed like a torture method or a recording Kim Jong-un would instruct be played at some mass rally in a gigantic square. Pretty soon, it came to feel as if someone had moved into the flat upstairs and was playing experimental jazz on a loop. Silence, cloying depressing silence, was better than this.

Down on the pitch – from where it must have sounded like a prison riot – I took immediately to Hibernian's centre-midfielder, Alex Gogić. Skin-headed and with socks rolled to his ankles, the Cypriot looked like the Bash Street Kid that the *Beano* forgot to draw. Early on, he blocked the ball's progress with such epic force that it made the noise of a crane dropping a steel rod from a great height. In a nearby old people's home, false teeth rattled in their bedside glasses of water. Minutes later, Gogić headed the ball so powerfully and loftily upwards that I expected a flock of passing geese to collapse from the sky.

As if in competition, the Aberdeen goalkeeper, Joe Lewis, thwacked a back-pass clearance almost perfectly vertically. It brought to mind the trajectory of the puck in a strongman game at a fairground as it surges towards the bell. Lewis wore a kit of bright yellow and enormous black gloves. From the far-flung press box, he resembled a bin man who had fled his round and now found himself on the pitch, just as a local cat might. For a good while, until he convinced me otherwise with a series of excellent saves, I kept expecting him to hurl the ball into the goal as if it were an escaped refuse sack and the net his wagon.

When at last the ball stayed on Earth for a while, Aberdeen should have scored. Striker Fraser Hornby was left alone on the penalty spot with the ball as if competing in a schools' half-time competition. One moment it was under his feet. The net was about to ripple, or at least quiver. The next, it was exiled by the touchline. It did not seem as if anyone had challenged him or won it, but that he had performed some kind of conjuring trick. This drama apparently silenced the fake home crowd; presumably somebody needed to turn the record over.

A while later, Hibs won a penalty. Lewis bashed both sets of studs six times on the foot of a post. It looked like some kind of stag mating ritual and made the sound of a mallet on scaffolding. Hibs' Martin Boyle remained unperturbed and scored. I wondered if my daughter was at the window.

An icy gust that scratched at cheeks whisked across the stadium. Hibs' marauding young left-back Josh Doig seemed to ride it as a surfer would a wave, bringing the ball with him. This outstanding local prodigy had made his debut on the first day of the season, thus never playing in front of supporters. I wondered how bereft he, and other new professionals like him, felt – no kid dreamed of turning out in front of empty seats or cardboard cut-outs of fans. Above that, their parents and loved ones would not have been there for a catalogue of firsts – first time on the bench, first substitute appearance, first full appearance, first goal…

Or had the lack of fans, with their hypercritical ways and bitter sniping, helped footballers like Doig? Might the return of supporters lessen their performance? That went too for other players, from the young to the veteran. Perhaps there was an arrogance about we supporters' collective view that football without us was nothing. Clearly some boo-boy targets must now be revelling, liberated from the tyranny of the barracking hordes and freed to play their game fearlessly. Behind-closed-doors football had inevitably altered the balance between home and away teams, statistics were beginning to prove that much; surely it had affected the way individuals played the sport too?

The second half began but I did not notice. I had entered some kind of trance in which my eyes fixed on the pitch but I saw nothing. Very possibly, the piped crowd noise had hypnotised me. The spirit of Romark was alive and well. As if flicking my ear, Gogić awoke me with a 50/50 hack at the ball that made the noise of a backfiring Lada. Soon afterwards, Aberdeen took a corner that swept its way over the penalty area and out for a goal-kick on the far side. It felt like a piece of eccentric performance art. A ball boy curved it back into play with what was to be the best pass of the game.

When we counted the ways in which we had missed football, the conversation often turned to particular players we could not wait to see again. No televised match or online feed allows the besotted scrutiny that being there does, nor the chance of interaction – him clapping for *you* as he leaves the field when substituted. We yearned to witness again how he truly moved, as is only possible in person. There were, too, signings we had never seen live, and some we never would – those Mary Poppins players who, during football's closed seasons, arrived on loan or on short-term contracts, did their jobs and then flew away.

Often, these pined-after players were creatives or forwards. Watching the Hibs centre-half Darren McGregor today made me think that, once fans were back, it was footballers like him that they would realise they had missed the most. The robust McGregor, born locally 35 years ago, played as if he would not only run through a brick wall for his team, but then return to rebuild it and run through it again. He was a heartbeat player, a stalwart who usually managed to muddy his shorts on the driest of afternoons and had a chest like the rump of a Highland cow. While he would often win the ball thunderously, McGregor should never be mistaken for a brute; he was capable of gliding out of defence and springing Hibs forward, the boxer poet. Once fans were back here, they would see him pursuing a visiting striker with the enthusiasm of a farm dog chasing a tractor and think: 'Boy, did I miss him.' Right on cue, he hacked a clearance that hung in the air like a flag.

Boyle scored again with a quarter of the game remaining, his shot careering through Lewis's legs like a bowling ball between skittles. The artificial ultras were momentarily silenced while a snippet of The Proclaimers' '500 Miles' was played. It reminded me of the moment ears finally unpop after a flight. Aberdeen looked dishevelled. The Dons were playing with all the passion of a man approving the back of his neck in a barber's hand mirror. They sent on substitute Shay Logan carrying a note on a folded-up piece of paper. He passed it to Andrew Considine, who seemed to read it for an unexpectedly long time. This indulged my long-held suspicion that such notes have nothing to do with football tactics, and are, say, meal options for the coach home or Shakespearean sonnets. Either way, Logan's energy and guile finally inspired Aberdeen to advance forward, but by then it didn't matter; he had arrived at the party bearing gifts, only to find an empty room and a caretaker sweeping up.

The sun fell and the wind whistled hauntingly, blowing lanyards up into the faces of their wearers. Seagulls hovered as they often did here towards the end of the game. For many months now, they must have wondered why the shoe-squashed chips and hot-dog butts, once their easy prey, had vanished. 'If you know your history/It's enough to make your heart go…' sang the invisible army as the referee executed the match.

In the dark abandoned streets below, with chanting tinnitus for accompaniment, I began to think that I had found all the stories I wanted to tell of behind-closed-doors football. My season would not continue until, in some form and anywhere, spectators were there too.

A fortnight after the Hibernian versus Aberdeen game, the suspended English non-league season was finally abandoned and whitewashed from history. The games and goals I'd seen at Lancaster, Workington and elsewhere no longer existed. Attendances and player appearance figures were annulled, expunged and redacted. More ghosts and shadow worlds had come to fruition.

It was time to close my eyes and believe in the spring.

8

24/04/21
Rothbury 5 v 1 Forest Hall
Team Valley Carpets Combination Cup

In some Northumbrian field, she ran alongside the train. A little girl of five or six, arms outstretched and waving. For a few seconds, those of us looking out of our carriage windows could see the wild exhilaration on her rosy face. The sun lit the scene and Britain was moving groggily and in stages out of lockdown. By late April, it was possible to feel optimistic without almost immediately feeling foolish.

Back in February, bulky snow had fallen and for a while distracted us. Those fortunate enough to be working from home could look out on to disguised streets and pretend the weather had stopped life, as opposed to a terrifying, incessant pandemic. For the lucky many who did not work on the margins of mayhem and were untouched by personal tragedy, there was an overriding emotion of boredom. Sheer, defeated, exhausted boredom.

A year ago, some had boasted of using their lockdown wisely to learn Japanese, bake bread heavier than a cannonball or perform lunges in front of a squawky man on television. Now when we made eye contact with one another, we saw nothing apart from dollops of resignation peppered with a smidgeon of vaccine-based hope.

Some, albeit not many, turned to resistance and conspiracy theories. My lonesome strolls improved immeasurably once I discovered the pleasure of spotting their graffiti. 'Social Distancing Is Profit For Big Tech' someone had scrawled in chalk capitals on a path through our local park, and then there was 'The masks don't work, Boris never had it' in crayon on the chipboard of a closed-down shop. Much sadder was a note in a window that read: 'I need a hug. It's been 365 days since I've felt the warmth of another human. Will wear a mask, shower – disinfect, clean clothes beforehand.'

When reading these declarations and witnessing other upsetting distortions over the past year, it had become possible to imagine that we had slipped into the pages of a science fiction novel. Such things will stay with us, especially the domestic minutiae: I will never forget one relative's fanatical cleaning of all fruit and vegetables, or another's conversion of a broom cupboard into a postal quarantine area for mail received. On my Mum's local high street, one man walked around holding a two-metre distancing stick aloft like a sword. The next generation of therapists will live in castles.

Through those winter months of early 2021, it was possible to detect a lethargy in football supporters too, or at least those of us following mid-table, mediocre teams. Repetition of a live feed ritual did not lead to the calming sense of fulfilment a matchday routine does. Months of watching empty seats and terraces, even partially covered in banners and cut-outs of fans, had become tiresome. Many talked of 'bingeing' Netflix series. Here was a form of on-screen entertainment we'd rather have nibbled on and then discarded. Absence from grounds had not just made the heart grow fonder, it had made some of us give up watching until we could be there again. Never had we been more aware of the fact that going to the match was about so much more than the going to the match. The nicotine patch of online access had stopped working.

Not that our overall love had been diminished. The bold, raging way we felt about the good that is in the game found expression when, in the third week of April 2021, a European Super League

(ESL) was proposed. The continent's richest and greediest clubs would flee their domestic competitions and play one another in a gluttonous joust of high revenues and no relegation. It was an extraordinary moment in an extraordinary time. Supporter opposition was vocal, militant and included devotees of the breakaway clubs. One by one, those clubs withdrew their applications, fat lords leaving the banquet as the peasants at the gate grew louder. Forty-eight hours after its announcement, the ESL collapsed. Some fans danced in the streets. Others raised a glass and gritted their teeth for next time. Anger did not melt – on the first Sunday in May, outraged Manchester United fans forced their way into Old Trafford and protested on the pitch. That afternoon's game with fellow ESL runaways Liverpool had to be postponed.

Those protests represented the first time that large congregations of supporters had gathered together in over a year. Outside Chelsea's Stamford Bridge and elsewhere, they wore their shirts and sang their songs, only there was no game to go to, and their placards spoke not to their teams but of how we all felt: 'Fans Not Customers', 'Football Belongs To Us Not You' and 'We Want Our Cold Nights In Stoke'. It would be another month before they sat and stood together again, but now tentative dates had been set. Christmas was coming but twice a year. For some, that would mean limited-capacity matches before the season's end. For others, watching ties at the European Championship. Then, by pre-season and when August came, we would all be back. We began to feel like the girl running alongside the train.

Whole worlds away from ESL largesse, English non-league clubs began to discuss the arrangement of 'Covid Cups' – short, localised tournaments that would give their players game time and allow supporters to attend. Many proposals fell away once it was realised that no fans would be allowed to watch in a ground at any level until the middle of May. Yet, from 17 April, nothing prevented small crowds assembling to watch matches played in public spaces. Suddenly, game-starved people found themselves standing in parks watching teams from the low steps of football.

If there was a perimeter fence, 22 players and a changing room block or clubhouse, it would do. More than that, it would make us smile.

Similarly ravenous, I scoured for fixtures and stumbled upon the Team Valley Carpets Combination Cup. It was to be competed by clubs from the Northern Alliance, a league constructed of teams from Northumberland, Tyneside, Wearside and County Durham. Three days after the implosion of the ESL, I set out on that train through Northumbria for Morpeth. From there, I would take a bus to Rothbury and watch a quarter-final between the home side and Forest Hall.

* * *

In Morpeth Bus Station, a vending machine had been refurbished to become Mask Box, offering a dozen or so different types of face covering and anti-bacterial hand gel. It all seemed very sensible, until later on when you fancied a KitKat and a bottle of Lilt. Classical music was being played over the station's speaker system. Brahms reached a triumphant climax while four teenage lads argued about how late the 35 to Pegswood would be, and a young goth girl looked at the long queue outside Subway, then whispered 'Eeeee, piss off' under her breath and walked away.

Arriva North East buses have mint-green livery and interiors. This hue even permeates their windows, bleeding across the glass in stickered form. Sitting on one is the closest most of us will come to living inside a tube of toothpaste. Today, looking across the X14 to the pleasant and rolling Northumbrian countryside felt like a psychedelic, LSD-fuelled experience as imagined by a member of Lindisfarne. I was still seeing in a strange colour when I alighted at Rothbury, as if an old-fashioned protective cellophane sheet from the window of a gentleman's outfitters had been pulled over my eyes. When later I passed two police officers, I became convinced that they were going to call me a beatnik and throw me in a van.

On Rothbury's Front Street, couples gazed at fire pokers and Tupperware in the window of T.W. Alderson & Sons ironmongery store. Opposite, children shook pocket-money change while deliberating in J.R. Soulsby & Sons toy shop. Up the hill on High Street, pensioners undertook the big toe test in Thomas Rogerson Shoes. The church bells rang, an old man in a suit dozed by the war memorial and it felt like Saturday afternoon inside a cosy period drama about a veterinary practice. This was a blissful little town.

A 2.30pm kick-off is, somehow, and to me anyhow, remarkably discombobulating. Walking back down High Street and out towards Rothbury F.C.'s Armstrong Park ground, I found myself quietly chanting the match itinerary like a dittery, hesitant mantra: '2.30 kick-off so 3.15 half-time. 3.30 second half... 4.15 full-time. But what if half-time is shorter? 2.30 kick-off, 3.15 half-time...' Obsessing over such things here was to miss the point; this was a timeless town, today's fixture a release and not a burden. I stepped left from a country road and on to a gravel track. At its conclusion was one of England's finest amphitheatres.

I had never seen a football venue like Armstrong Park. It was a terraced Eden, the missing stanza in Blake's 'Jerusalem' – a green and pleasant ground. A wide grass pathway delivered visitors at a cutting between mounds. On each side, daffodils took the places of stewards, their petals fluorescent jackets. From there, the pitch and its surroundings unfolded as if in the palm of an opening hand.

That pitch was luscious, its broad stripes appearing to shimmer in the sun. Along one touchline ran a mass of trees, now coming to life after a winter's slumber. They curved around the far corner and as far as the goal, at which point a giant sycamore towered over them and seemed to halt their progress. A steady hill grew behind it, sweeping around and running the length of the sideline, and then back to the cutting. Such were its gradients to the pitch, it looked every inch a terrace from some 1930s photograph, transported from an inner-city club, landed here and then reclaimed by nature, its flat-capped fans replaced by farmers' sons and poachers. After the cutting, it continued, so that 20 or so viewers were able to stand at the top of this wild kop. Here was an eco-stadium before its time, and a dream in which football had become a genteel rural pursuit.

In the days prior to the fixture, Rothbury had announced plans to redevelop Armstrong Park. Where usually that can be cause for scepticism and panic, the scheme here was for improved clubhouse facilities and the installation of floodlights. In keeping with the basic, bucolic feeling of the ground, I hoped that these might be made from giant candles or modelled on coastal fire beacons.

Rothbury – or, the Hillmen – were founded in 1876 but did not move to Armstrong Park until 1949. In their early years of life here, the Hillmen would each summer host Newcastle United. After the Magpies won the FA Cup in 1955 – their most recent domestic honour – they brought the trophy to the game and then paraded it in the town. It is, as such, probable that the legendary Jackie Milburn played on this field. Another Ashington great, Bobby Charlton, also kicked a ball beneath the grassy knolls, when playing for Northumberland County Juniors. This place must constitute the most unchanged arena in which either maestro competed, an untouched conservation area of a venue where only the players themselves need be left to the imagination.

Spectators roved through the cutting and settled on the shelf halfway up the pastoral terrace, a natural separation between upper and lower tiers. A toddler ran around and his mam urged him to greet the men in all-red: 'There's your uncle. And there's Dad, number 6. Wave back to him.' Two men in their early twenties arrived together and found a bench to sit on. With a kitchen bin close by, and access to a dog bowl brimming with water, this position constituted today's executive offering.

More people materialised from the far side, emerging out of a forest and negotiating a stile to do so. They resembled explorers, creeping from the jungle and stumbling on this lost civilisation of running men with studded feet, giant net dreamcatchers and spears in every corner.

The Hillmen's opponents, Forest Hall from north Newcastle, wore the faint blue shirts and black shorts and socks of Uruguay.

Crows sat on branches, clicking and cawing like avian ultras. 'Come on lads', 'Keep it simple' and 'Watch that bounce', replied the humans on the pitch. The referee counted the players and I counted the watchers. Around 50 had arrived now, a crowd that would be supplemented throughout the afternoon by passing dog walkers and hikers, and at one point a man who drove in and asked me, mysteriously, if I knew where he could find a river.

This earthy amphitheatre cushioned noise made on the pitch and echoed back a muffled version. The studs of a group of players chasing the same ball came to sound like wild horses stomping across a prairie. These surroundings must have seemed strange to those visiting Geordies who had not played at Armstrong Park before. As many of them looked to be teenage, that number could well have been high; I could imagine them returning home that night and saying excitedly, 'Mam, we played in a massive green crater today.'

Bamboozlement might account for the play of one such gangly tyke, apparently a defender. At times, this young Forest Hall man looked as if he wished someone would call him in for his tea. Then, he would reanimate and power into life like he was a fruit machine that had just been plugged in. On one occasion, he contrived to perform both roles within the same passage of play. Having jinked his way around three Rothbury men, he stopped and stood completely still in the manner of someone who had just been given bad news. The home side purloined the ball, but it then ricocheted back to him. At that point, he danced by another two opponents before lining up a shot, which he seemed to lose interest in as his leg swung towards the ball. It missed the target, but by then he appeared to have spotted something in the wooded mountains far beyond Armstrong Park.

At this level of the game, the physique of footballers varies tremendously. The professional sport now factory-farms a muscular breed and few players are matchstick runts or beanpole ogres. Down here, teams are a mix of the lanky, the lithe and the podgy. Some look like firemen and some chimney sweeps. A squad resembles a randomly selected jury rather than a finely-honed unit. For Rothbury, that meant the pairing up front of wiry Greg Woodburn with the burlier Paul Dunn.

Woodburn's craft and Dunn's power gnawed away at Forest Hall all afternoon. Early on, they harried the away defence into a tatty clearance that alienated their goalkeeper, so that he was now far from home. Woodburn flicked the stray ball to Dunn and he scored. Down on the shelf they held babies in the air and cheered. More families had arrived now, and parents nudged prams up and down the earthen terrace. It came to sound like a village fête with added cries of 'Man on!' and 'Hard lines!'

These surroundings and the atmosphere they nurtured made it hard to imagine any needle on the field of play. It was impossible to envisage two-footed tackles or 20-man brawls. Such events would be like swearing in front of someone's grandma. Today's linesmen were substitutes from each team, and yet there would not be a moment of dispute all afternoon.

Armstrong Park conditions may also explain why both teams dared to try to pass the ball out of defence from goal-kicks: there was no chance of any spectator here impolitely inducing players to 'Just bloody well lump it' as happened everywhere else, including in the Premier League. It was almost a relief when, during the usual turbulence of a penalty area prior to a corner being taken, opponents began to nudge and prod each other. 'Eeeee, cut it out!' shouted a man behind the goal. 'Aye, hands off, lads,' agreed the referee. From the corner, a shot flew in, span up through the cutting and slapped against the side of a car, setting off its alarm. 'Canny rowdy it is here today,' said a man near me. Soon after, Rothbury scored again and the carnival crowd whooped and whistled as if someone had just announced that raffle tickets were now half price.

Forest Hall rallied with the frantic zeal of someone collecting dry washing from a line as raindrops began to fall. They ran at the home side and lavished shots on the Rothbury goal. Each was met by the superb home goalkeeper, who had an athletic way of pawing away the ball with both hands that brought to mind the

Birdy Dance. He had rolled up his sleeves and wore black gloves, the cuffs of which stretched close to his elbows. When he plucked the ball from the air at set-pieces, it looked as though a mischievous old-fashioned chauffeur had invaded the pitch.

The goalkeeper also commanded his players in a style I had never heard before. As a Forest Hall winger shaped to cross, he would shout: 'That doesn't come in.' Then, when an opponent ran at a full-back: 'He doesn't turn you.' As a forward approached goal, there was even an: 'He doesn't score here.' Perhaps he could see into the future. I wondered what this new linguistic tense should be called – predictive goalkeeper? – and reflected that it reminded me of when our daughter was a toddler, and we would say things like 'No, we don't throw the plastic mug at Daddy, do we?'

The away side's surge wound down when one of their forwards tried to dribble around the Rothbury left-back but instead contrived to maim him. I missed the offending action as a rambler had appeared and stood precisely in front of me while looking at something through his binoculars. Five minutes later, he was still limping with the exaggerated hobble of a child playing a wounded soldier in a school play. The Rothbury left-back, that is.

Half-time brought open-air team talks and the scent of liniment drifting on the breeze. It felt disconcertingly urban – surely there was a manure-based muscle rub that could be used instead? The teams toddled back on to the pitch after a break of only five minutes, once again spinning my brain into a state of befuddlement. As the game recommenced, a dog yapped with the monotonous repetition of an unstoppable alarm clock. Perhaps it was trying to outsing the crows ('Who's the bastard in the black?').

With a chatty peace restored, I looked around at those others present. I wondered what part this game played in their lives, and how much they had missed it, or at least worried about their loved ones that it meant so much to. The two on the bench had remained and were now deep in conversation about their beloved Newcastle United. Close to me, a man took photographs of the game on an expensive camera, every now and then looking back at the little images on his tiny screen, then smiling slightly or shaking his head and trying again. There was a woman in her seventies, smartly dressed and looking on with a dose of grand-mother's pride welded across her face. Young lads in hoodies and shorts mucked around, grabbed each other in headlocks and tried to balance footballs in the rigid angle of their feet and shins. There was a family sitting on a blanket, picnic primed. Over on the kop, a dozen men and half a dozen women looked out, talking always and laughing often. Most will have known or been related to a player or two, and so here was the family, doing again what it should do.

All were soon cheering anew. Woodburn once again located Dunn. Dunn seemed to drag himself clear of the Forest Hall defence through raw willpower. With a soft touch he primed the ball as if garnishing a silver service main dish, hung back his foot and whacked it into a wincing net. Ten minutes later, Dunn cushioned and occupied the ball like a hero holding a lowering barrier so that others could escape underneath. Visiting players hacked and scraped at him but he could not be moved. When Woodburn arrived, Dunn rolled him the ball and he lashed it in, a favour returned. 'Is that four or five?' asked the Rothbury goalkeeper of his undisturbed defence.

Rothbury increasingly played an exhibitionist type of football as a team 4-0 up in the sunshine should. There were cross-park switches and nippy one-touch drills that seemed to trim the grass. Dunn tried a volley with the outside of his boot from 20 yards. Whatever the level of football, such play makes the spectator believe in this game all over again. It was not merely this unexpected artistry that made me feel oddly exhilarated for a man sitting alone in a pile of leaves; it was the rare sense that I did not wish to be anywhere else but here, now. That is a feeling to be treasured and a feeling football gives often, something I had forgotten.

A Rothbury centre-half tried a shot from distance, which was saved by the admirably persistent Forest Hall goalkeeper. The defender looked to the sidelines and asked: 'Dad, surely I'm getting a pint for that?' Before a reply could be gathered, Woodburn slipped the ball to Dunn and he scored again, a hat-trick accomplished. The Rothbury keeper looked to his manager and begged: 'Please, just put us up front.' Perhaps he'd had a premonition of scoring – 'He does score here.' Instead, he was taken off to allow his understudy a few minutes on the pitch. He ran on, spanked the crossbar and smashed his gloves together. It made the noise of a rug being beaten on a wall. He did not have much to do, other than stoop to collect Forest Hall's consoling penalty from the goal.

Soon, smaller lads climbed on the shoulders of larger teammates and performed the circus act of gathering nets. Talk turned to after-game drinks and semi-finals reached. Suddenly, lockdown was just a word and the beautiful nonsense that millions of us revelled in had ascended once more.

Back in town, early evening drinkers shuffled into the Turk's Head pub, where Newcastle's FA Cup had once gone on display. Next door, among the gleaming chrome frying ranges and heavenly smells of the fish shop, a laminated sign listed opening times for 'Lockdown 3.6'. I sat on a bench eating golden chips and drinking dandelion and burdock among tulips and muscari. A birdsong serenade began and church bells pealed.

* * *

A few days later I was back at my mum's house. From the hallway, she gestured towards the lounge and said, 'It's in there.' Pushing the door open revealed an upright object clad in bubble wrap, which I tore at. 'This reminds me of Christmas when you were a boy,' said Mum. And there it was: a beautiful old wooden seat from the main stand at York City's Bootham Crescent ground.

On the seat's backrest and underneath, varnish had been chiselled away by time and the elements. Both were now the colour of a pinecone. A number 13 was painted in an authoritative font on the paisley burls in the wood. It was possible to imagine many fans arriving, over the 80 years that this seat was in use, each in the clothes of their time, clocking this number and responding with a variation of: 'Oh. Seat number 13. We'll lose today, then.' That led to thoughts of the legions who had sung, sworn, cursed, bawled and leaped up to celebrate a goal from that very perch. They were part of its weathering too.

The panel that they would have rested their backsides on remained glossy and was the shade of Lyle's Golden Syrup. The seat's curvaceous brass bracket arms were corroding and rough to the touch. Bobbly stencilled words poked out of them but were indecipherable, the extrovert version of weathered gravestone etchings. Raising the seat on its joints, it made an amiable groan in the fashion of a person of a certain age getting up from a low-set armchair. My daughter, crouched next to me, moved it up and down so that this sound started and stopped in the same way she did with her first musical jewellery box.

These seats became available, for £60, because York were selling off Bootham Crescent, their bedraggled and charming city centre home. I wished they weren't, and that this antique was staying where it belonged. However, the demolition of the ground had been plotted for years. This was a heart-breaking tale of mismanagement and decay. The Minstermen were about to move to a bland out-of-town stadium. Houses would be built on cherished land where footballers had played, with car parks supplanting terraces. That had been a storyline for 30 years in Britain, and now there was a Covid-era subplot: clubs moving out of their worshipped homes without supporters being given the chance to say goodbye. Alongside York's midnight fleeing of Bootham Crescent, there could be no ceremony at Brentford's Griffin Park and no goodbye tears at Boston United's York Street.

Setting out from my mum's flat, I walked across town to the Crescent to say a private farewell. If it were possible, then being inside an abandoned stadium that would *never* reopen would epitomise pandemic-era football with its aura of absence and space. We had all, it seemed to me, missed our grounds as much as we had missed our teams. For followers of York – and Brentford and Boston – there would be no reunion.

Though born on Teesside and a slave to Middlesbrough F.C., my family moved to a village near York when I was a child. The Minstermen became my 'second team', which can often be an odd, ambiguous relationship. It is an almost embarrassing phrase to use, with its connotations of disloyalty or greed – one club is just not enough. That is if we even use those words; usually we'll just say things like 'I go to watch York sometimes too' or 'York are my soft-spot team'. It is difficult for us to don these second clubs' shirts. Even a scarf can sit uncomfortably and seem to make your neck itch, or give the feeling of wearing an item of clothing borrowed from someone else. First-game memories are not as clear or lionised – I *think* my York debut was a victory over a team in white, possibly Hereford, possibly Fulham.

Yet I remember the wooden seats and have clear memories of how Bootham Crescent looked and felt and smelled in the 1990s. Most of them are floodlit. There was the exhilarating capacity crowd squash of a victorious play-off game against Bury in 1993. Then play-offs in the division above the following season, and soon after seeing through an aggregate victory over Manchester United in the Coca-Cola Cup, Cantona's stiff collar and all. The next year, we saw York beat Everton here in the same competition, and then invaded the oily pitch, berserk teenagers with no thoughts of double chemistry in the morning. Then on one December Saturday towards the end of the century came the slaying, in a league game, of Manchester City. Afterwards, they moved gradually towards the stratosphere and the Minstermen to near oblivion.

With the Minster bells at my back, I walked the same old route for the very last time, out of the embrace of the York Walls and along Bootham. Blossom trees bled confetti petals on handsome Grosvenor Street, always an unlikely football thoroughfare with its three-storey villas and B&Bs. It was from here that you would first hear matchday – indistinct tannoy rasps and bursts of 'We are York' and 'Oh to be a Yorkie' from the terraces of the David Longhurst Stand. Those sounds would

quicken the pace of the people around you, as if they were workers scuttling towards the factory bell. At the end of Grosvenor,
other supporters would flow down from what many called 'the
Monkey Bridge', quickly negotiating its steps with their hands
in their pockets, then looking up to find that Bootham Crescent
was now in view. They would walk past a queue of us younger
fans waiting to buy pop and sweets at the newsagent on the
corner. That shop was now bricked up, the first act of erasure
among the coming many. A glance down the back-to-backs of
Newborough Street brought flashed recall of Tony's Plaice, a
glowing chippy it was possible to visit at half-time by collecting
a 'pass out' chit from a steward.

From there we had looked towards the gates of Bootham
Crescent and melted into the matchday whirlpool. Now, the
ground had been stripped of its signs, unscrewed or claw-
hammered and then auctioned to fans. With faded squares and
rectangles where directions, gate prices and codes of conduct
had been displayed, it looked as if the place had been suddenly
censored. Behind the away end, where buddleia leaned over the
perimeter wall like misbehaving fans, I ran my hand down a
turnstile door frame and paint peeled away. Hours later, red and
blue fragments remained in my fingernails.

The club shop resembled any other empty retail unit, with no
trace of besotted post-game moments when cash had been parted
with for anything that said 'York City' on it. Two men moved
cardboard boxes from the programme shop to a car boot. I asked
where their contents were going. 'Tip, I'm afraid, son,' came the
reply. We chatted for a while about programmes, about York City
and Bootham Crescent, and about the £1 programme bundles I
used to buy from them in my teens. They gave me another pile
now, for old times' sake.

By the main stand, near to the door we would wait outside
for player autographs, was a heap of flags, banners and poles,
extracted from the stands and left for dead. Beyond them, two
men in club apparel were heaving rows of plastic seats into a van.

The wide double-door gate into the ground behind them was open. 'Excuse me,' I said, possibly in the voice of a child asking to see Santa, 'can I go in?' Without looking up, the older of the two replied, 'Aye. If you're careful.'

This magic house unfurled before me. I stood first behind the goal in the Longhurst Stand, recalling aloft arms and kids stretching on tiptoes to see the action on those glory nights. Pigeons cooed rowdily and the grass was long and unkempt, but it remained possible to trick ears into hearing the sounds of yesterday, and to look to the pitch and see bygone happenings, or at the columns of crush barriers around me and rekindle faces from a quarter of a century ago. The men drove their van across it, and the smell of diesel momentarily stopped my being homesick for the past.

At the back of the stand, the snack bar shutter was bolted forever, its meal deal signs intact. Never again would anyone Choose Any Pie with Any Hot or Soft Drink for £5.50. Many advertising hoardings had been removed, which regressed the look of some parts of the ground even further back than I remembered. Elsewhere, the peeling away of modern adverts had unveiled older boards. There was one for York City Clubcall, and another for Warner Brothers' 'new' cinema in an out-of-town retail park, which was, as I recall it, the most exciting thing to happen in 1990 apart from the World Cup. Moss advanced up breeze-block walls like storm clouds on a television weather map and I began to wonder if seeing – and in future recalling – the dear old place in this state was such a good idea.

Here I was, though, and only in this instant could I snoop inside the decomposing wooden hut where supporters would pay £1 to transfer into the seats of the Popular Stand, or sneak beneath that same enclosure to look at the long access tunnel, which had been used as an air-raid shelter in the war. Without paying my pound, I continued on and into the 'Pop', with its alphabet steps denoting rows now gagged and smothered by dandelions and other trespassing weeds. Inside a unit cupboard, a meter box, used to record how many people had paid their money and passed through, remained stuck on 11. A few blocks on, the two men removed further rows of seats. They had been reserved by clubs in Birtley, Penistone, Galashiels and Warrington. With so many parts of the ground sold off and sent around the country, there would be corners of fields that were forever Bootham Crescent, a scattering of the ashes.

I looked across to the main stand, now robbed barren and flashing a boxer's tooth-scarce grin, most of its wooden seats in living rooms and elsewhere. Moving close up – not across the pitch, I'd leave that sensation firmly in 1996 – brought sight of that area's internal organs, its concrete steps, nuts and bolts and shady warrens. Like many Middlesbrough fans, I had watched fever-ishly as our new Riverside Stadium was built in the mid-nineties, visiting regularly and witnessing its construction in stages. Today, it was possible to see the inner workings of Bootham Crescent through its slow destruction, an intriguing but grim encounter. I stood at the players' tunnel looking outwards, a vantage I'd only had once before, when selected as a matchday ballboy aged 13. Such is the way this game lands the adult back in smaller shoes.

Pushing at slender doors, I found discarded sports equipment and a long forgotten W.T. Ellison turnstile, its counter aban-doned at 50185. Back by the pitch, a blackbird pecked at the cleft which once hosted a corner flag's pole, and a thousand stud marks remained, the fossils of linesmen and substitutes. For a while I rested on a crush barrier in the away end, looking out and wondering how many thousands of people down the years had called this place home. Now, the clocks had stopped and I was standing in a memory.

I walked along the fading touchline, reached the corner and had one last look around. Outside, the older man asked: 'You all done, son?' I said I was, but he probably knew that much by the tears in my eyes.

9

Billingham Synthonia 0 v 2 West Auckland Town
Durham Challenge Cup Final

A rousing hymn played and as usual the congregation joined in for its chorus. That refrain was all most of them knew, but still 'Abide With Me' handed over the reward of goosebumps. In living rooms and pubs, lovers of English football hummed through the verses and felt simultaneously uplifted and like crying away all the grief and frustration of the past 14 months.

What made this rendition of the song seep with poignancy was that supporters were there. For the 2021 FA Cup final, 21,000 of them had been allowed into Wembley. It was the biggest crowd any of us had seen since we first heard the words 'You must stay at home'. From sofas and bar stools, we listened to this stuffy anthem of our youth and rejoiced. It felt like a siren heralding the end of the old times and the beginning of the new, an ice-cream van chasing away ambulances. We could only imagine how good it must have felt for those Chelsea and Leicester City supporters inside the stadium. *Shine through the gloom and point me to the skies…*

Many of us hardly watched the early parts of the game. We sat in agreeable distraction, looking into the stands at fans in their seats. It seemed like an optical illusion, and that if we moved the television they might disappear in the manner of a hologram. For so long, the background to matches had been plastic and concrete; now it was tiny figures in their scarves, rising and falling, arms applauding or gesticulating.

The noise struck us too. After so much fakery or hush, it seemed intensely raw and vital. The soundscape had graduated swiftly from that of an unintelligibly quiet radio in a dental surgery to the zest and bedlam of a punk gig. It made the game itself more vivid and urgent. Round-mouthed 'Oooooh' noises looped around Wembley when either team went close to a goal. Guttural yowls fell down in torrents after poor tackles or perceived refereeing mistakes. Such noises seemed to make the match crisper and more meaningful than any we had watched in a year. Then Leicester's Youri Tielemans hit a 25-yard whizbanger into the top corner and we remembered what a goal was supposed to sound like.

The FA Cup final had been among a series of 'test events' plucked from various sports to gauge how crowds might safely be readmitted to venues. It took place on 15 May, two days before wider rule relaxations in England began. As part of those changes, limited numbers of fans would be able to attend any remaining fixtures, or indeed friendly or cup ties that could be hastily arranged. Watching EFL play-off games with their scattered but vociferous attendees in the ground made a throbbing spectacle from a damp squib. Screen disillusion retreated. Enthusiasm and optimism bloomed. Cruel cold reality, though, lurked in the background as usual – another new Covid variant, Delta, was beginning to spread quickly through the country. Further, subsequent freedoms would be postponed until later in the summer.

In non-league football, clubs saw an opportunity. Though leagues had been abandoned, from 17 May supporters could be welcomed in to watch games in tournaments that had spent much of the season hibernating. One such competition was the Durham County FA Challenge Cup, first played in 1884. Four days after football's reawakening at Wembley, Billingham Synthonia would face West Auckland Town for this year's trophy. It was, very probably, the last chance I would have to enjoy the redemption of a crowd in this uncommon and tumultuous season.

That fine Wednesday afternoon, the North Sea glimmered when lumpy clouds were not forcing the sun into a game of peek-a-boo. Holy Island looked closer than it does during dismal weather, a trick of the light and another dividend of this beautiful streak of railway line. As if extinguishing such feeble thoughts, a train cleaner wearing a *Ghostbusters*-style backpack squished the air with anti-bacterial spray. It made the carriage smell like the inside of a hospital broom cupboard.

At Newcastle station, last September's giddy drinkers had been replaced by a stream of black-and-white crusaders. For the only time this season, some Newcastle United supporters would be able to watch their team from the vertiginous stands of St James' Park. Scarves had been yanked from pegs and shaken free of dust, and now pubs and other places of matchday ritual would be encountered again. In towns and cities across the land, old habits were being revived.

There, I changed to a train bound for Teesside and that evening's game. As ever, Northern Rail had supplied an old diesel locomotive that smelled like a fire in a cheese-and-onion crisp factory and seemed to start up as if coughing for attention. Its interior fittings had been refurbished, an optimistic gesture that fooled nobody. On the horizon, the River Tyne's last industrial cranes stood guarding their river. Closer by, wild horses galloped madly away from the train as if they had read the dreaded words 'Northern Rail'. We skirted Jarrow F.C.'s Perth Green home and the Scotch Estate, triggering thoughts of that first game back, which seemed to have been both an event from only last week and a vaguely recalled memory from the last century. At the table across from mine, a teenager began to rap in an accent that was half-Bronx and half-Hebburn. He rhymed 'snitches' with 'bitches' and I sat tight, anticipating a verse about unpleasant itches and irrigation ditches.

This coastal line that trundled through Wearside, County Durham and Teesside was one I knew well. All the same, I had not travelled here since late 2019 so that changes were obvious, as when immediately spotting the growth in a friend's child and then annoying that child by insisting on mentioning it. In Sunderland, City Hall, two stout blocks not unlike giant stickle-brick pieces, now occupied a perch high on the riverbank near the Wearmouth Bridge. During the periods when travel was largely limited, places had stayed the same in our minds but not in reality. There were also temporary changes – each locality with its Covid slogans and graphics, strewn in the air on banners or grounded in two-metre space markers, a nightmare shared across the globe but tailored by local marketing departments.

Outside Seaham, the rapping teen announced that he was 'Off for a tab in the bogs'. The tarry stench startled a Train Safety Officer into action. As we languished near Seaham Station, it was impossible not to hear the resulting confrontation. I tried to look out of the window and concentrate on the game under way at Seaham Harbour Cricket Club, which meant their conversation became something of a commentary. A lanky bowler sped towards the crease just as the rapper pleaded that it was 'only a cheeky rollie'. It was a bit like a north-eastern version of *Test Match Special*.

They were soon drowned out by the retching of the locomotive's engine and three friends in their early twenties. Their pent-up laughter at nothing in particular cut the tension and filled the air merrily. The train now flanked the North Sea, rendered almost invisible by an abrupt mizzle. 'Looks like the end of the Earth, that,' said a man behind me. 'How would you bloody know?' replied a woman whose exasperated, curt tone indicated that they were husband and wife. 'You never go anywhere.'

Soon, the train was panting through Teesside, industry clawing its way around the distant mouth of the mighty River Tees. How I had missed this cluttered industrial skyline of pipes, towers and great steel spires. 'It's too spicy for me, this,' commented flat-Earth man about a sandwich he had opened. 'Course it bloody is,' said his wife, loaded with years of marital contempt. 'A cup of tea's too spicy for you.'

We passed through Billingham, with its cooling towers in the background and orderly pre-fabricated post-war bungalows by the railway line. Tonight's game would be played here alongside the tracks, at the home of Billingham Town, Bedford Terrace. With time to spare, I went first for a walk around Stockton-on-Tees, the adjoining, larger town in which I was born but hardly knew.

* * *

All was silent in sparse Stockton station, a place that does not make enough of its role in the birth of the railways, as if trying to avoid a clip round the ear for showing off. Outside a nearby parade of shops, a woman placed two fingers to her lips and whistled vigorously towards an upstairs window, a modern-day knocker-up. I fell in behind two other women as they left a pub. Various pedestrian crossings and different turns meant that we repeatedly crossed paths while walking to the town centre. This resulted in my overhearing segments of a long monologue about some leather trousers, and then the magnificent line: 'The thing is, I sound tall on the phone, if you know what I mean.'

Sometimes a building stops your progress as if two magnets have collided. It is asking to be looked at in the same way a peacock showing its feathers seems to be. The Stockton Globe theatre, a newly refurbished Art Deco wonder, did just that. Its beauty sparkled in the late afternoon sun. After years of dereliction, this sweet northern rose of a place was soon to reopen. Its rejuvenation also had the effect of rekindling glint-eyed tales from the past; local stories about the names who had once played there, from Buddy Holly to The Rolling Stones. One relative had recently told me how The Beatles had been here on the day John F. Kennedy was assassinated. Scheduled to play two shows, they were informed of the news after the first, and decided to continue and play their evening set too.

The Globe poses at the end of England's widest high street. 'It's wider than yours/It's wider than yours' sing followers of Stockton Town F.C. to the tune of 'Sloop John B': 'Stockton High Street/It's wider than yours.' Landscaped and polished up in recent years, and with its Victorian town hall at the centre, it is prettier than most too. There is also a sculpture that nods to railway history, the *Stockton Flyer*, though in keeping with the hush-hush approach to that topic, its kinetic locomotive rises up and appears just once a day. The rest of the time there is only an empty plinth. Much more adamant are the fountains that incessantly pitter-patter like a jungle monsoon.

As market stall owners hauled down the scaffold frames of their stalls, three women poured from a taxi, their arms aloft. 'We're out, and we're staying out,' shouted one. Here was a happy sight to encounter – people, shedding the misery of the year they had lived, heartily indulging in those things they had missed, just as many of us wished to do with football.

Booming music spurted out of pubs. Outside the Clock Tower bar, half a dozen men in cowboy western-wear drew on fags as if seeking adrenaline for an impending showdown. Karaoke warbling seeped from the window of the John Walker Tavern. Walker was an esteemed son of Stockton who accidentally invented the friction match, then waived his patent due to a desire that it be used freely to help liberate the poor. Attempts at commemoration beyond the pub's name had not been successful. In 2001, a sculpture of two large matches was installed at the centre of a roundabout but proved unpopular and was subsequently removed. Then a bust of Walker, commissioned in 1977 and on display in town since, turned out to be based on a portrait of the wrong man entirely.

Beneath an alluring 1960s typeface announcing Pearl Assurance House, a lightbox in the window of the Accetto café urged: 'Got To Love Your Parmesan'. The Parmesan – or, more commonly, 'Parmo', a breaded chicken or pork breast saturated in bechamel sauce and then blanketed in cheese – had become something of a cultural touchstone on Teesside over the previous few decades. The late, great local radio commentator Alistair Brownlee's cry of 'Everybody round my house for a parmo!' following victory in a UEFA Cup semi-final adorns a wall next to the Riverside Stadium. Now parmos were spreading to takeaways across the land and had appeared on *MasterChef*, I wondered if another regional speciality, the London Pizza – a pizza topped with chips – might catch on next. Hoardings by Accetto's promised yet more improving change here; soon, a decrepit shopping mall and hotel would be bulldozed, and a new park built. That would open the high street to the River Tees. Stockton is a place on the turn.

Down a colourful alleyway, where each shop or house was painted in pastel colours as if a part of Mexico had hopped here and decided to stay, I found the snug Golden Smog pub. My pint tasted so good that it could only have been matchday.

* * *

The train back to Billingham shunted past Bedford Terrace. Players in luminous bibs jogged around in yolky sunlight and a dozen people had already occupied spaces upon the main stand's wooden benches. Kick-off was 45 minutes away, but those minutes were merely a short countdown after so much time without grounds to go to.

Stepping down from the carriage at Billingham Station, I was immediately engulfed in a thick smog. It covered the platform and the two tracks it strafed. I half expected my daughter to run towards me through the smoke shrieking 'Daddy, my Daddy!' Soon it transpired that a barbecue in a neighbouring garden had gone awry and its emissions now engulfed much of the surrounding area.

Through streets of tidy semi-detached homes, I followed signs for Billingham Town F.C. and then I saw them – a hundred or more people, walking towards a ground in that familiar and yet part-forgotten manner, full of intent and purpose. Some looked ahead and let modest smirks form across their faces. Others had their heads down as if awaiting the surprise. They were walking into the floodlights and the sun and away from the life we had lived.

Close to the ground, a boy leaned his bike against a fence and sat on its crossbar, watching the scene as if the fair was arriving in town. In front of him was a large cardboard placard, gaffer-taped on to a plastic parking barrier. In marker pen it declared 'Players & Officials Only', with the 'Only' underlined twice, a power of emphasis and enforcement long held by committee men up and down the land. I would have put them in charge of Covid branding and messaging. Very few people disobey a double-underlined rule written in old man's capitals.

Among the potholes and threadbare tarmac of the car park, we queued at the turnstile, its rattles loudening and ratcheting up with each slow step forward. We were at, and arguably beyond, the traditional end to a season, yet the tone of chatter now was more of the optimistic, nigh on cock-a-hoop type familiar in August. It wasn't that people talked specifically of the game ahead, more that their moods were high and they were imbued with the sense that this was the start of something. Closing in, masks were raised and track and trace duties performed. The pandemic was always ready to tap us on the shoulder.

On the other side, they raised their arms to their foreheads to fend off the sun and looked to the pitch. The players of Billingham Synthonia – or 'Synners' – and West Auckland Town did their final stretches and drills before retreating to the dressing rooms, always in groups of three or four and always animated in conversation or laughing. This was not a social sport for the spectators alone. Middle-aged men with plastic bags holding flasks and spare layers watched as kids in full kits played mini games of their own. On a table, the Durham Challenge Cup stood quite alone, an elaborate piece of silverware whose handles looked like the wings of an exotic moth. Sunlight bounced from its bulbous chest and for a moment it looked as if the resultant ray was about to open some lost and ancient portal as in an adventure film about Aztecs.

I bent down to read the names inscribed on its footplate. An old man with handsome eyes and a flat cap joined me and began to read out loud: 'Oh aye, Hartlepools have won it. Spennymoor. Consett, aye. I remember that one. 1969. If you go way back, son, Sunderland used to win it regular. *The* Sunderland. Mind, they won every bugger back then. They'd not even beat Billingham now.' He chuckled to himself and walked away, having reminded me of football's cosmic power to make strangers momentarily and enrichingly familiar. Further, it reaffirmed the feeling that the locking of the turnstiles closed to many an opportunity for company, no matter how fleeting or apparently superficial.

Bedford Terrace crackled in the minutes before kick-off that evening. In the short but deep main stand, and on the terraces and grass banks that ran until they met the busy homespun shack opposite, there was a sense of occasion. With that beautiful Victorian trophy on display, and local FA blazers pottering with intent, it was even possible to discern an air of formality. This represented a surprisingly refreshing phenomenon in a time when none of us had had occasion to wear our smart clothes in months.

The teams jogged out and a young tannoy voice welcomed us all back to 'Real, live football', a pronouncement cheered by some who gathered on the picnic benches outside the social club and raised their pint pots in salute. Being able to watch a match from that position with those refreshments to hand seemed to me the very height of civilisation.

As they fell into their shape before kick-off, Synthonia's green and white quarters seemed to shine in the way a photograph does when held beneath a lightbulb. Their poetic surname is actually a portmanteau of 'Synthetic Ammonia', an agricultural fertiliser made in Billingham since the club was founded in the 1920s. For a long time, this was a works town and that works was a sprawling collection of ICI factories and plants whose incandescent flues seemed to set the night sky aflame. Though ICI may be no more, its team remains, as do the Synthonia cricket club and Scout

164

groups. The town's chemical legacy continues, and as we stood watching this match, workers at a nearby factory were developing a new Covid vaccine, Novavax. West Auckland Town, meanwhile, lined up in the same black and yellow colours they had worn while winning the 'World Cup' twice.

In 1909, the Scottish tea magnate Sir Thomas Lipton announced that he would fund and help organise an international football tournament in Italy. Although keen on the game and in developing calcio in that country, Lipton also appears to have had a beady awareness of the marketing potential of this growing sport. The Glaswegian, and his Italian co-organisers at *La Stampa* newspaper, decreed that the competition should be held in Turin. A combined team of players from local sides Torino and Piemonte would represent Italy, with Stuttgart appearing on behalf of Germany and Winterthur for Switzerland.

West Auckland were a team of miners – skilful but ragtag amateurs from the Northern League. For years, a yarn was spun that they had been invited by mistake; Lipton and the Italians had intended to contact another 'WA' football club, Woolwich Arsenal. However, a recent book, *The Miners' Triumph*, vanquished this rumour and proved that those in Turin knew very well that they had contacted and would be receiving a volunteer club from England's rugged north.

In their eyes, most British teams played to a similar standard, one good enough to compete and prosper in Italy. The book's author, Martin Connolly, quoted a report in *La Stampa*: 'If we claimed the English team that will compete in our tournament is the best from foggy Britain, it would be presumptuous and maybe even foolish. In fact, in a country where thousands and thousands of football clubs are flourishing, you cannot categorically claim to be a team that is a cut above the rest.' Their hope was that the presence of this particular 'elite group of champions from the land of Albion' would inspire locals and raise the Italian game.

West needed donations from local businesses to fund their squad's travel. Even that was not enough; some players sold personal possessions to ensure they could afford a train from Darlington to Turin Porta Nuova. They must have felt it was worthwhile. The Italians' lofty assessment of English football's universal prowess seemed accurate: the north-easterners defeated the Germans 2-0 in the semi-final, and the Swiss by the same scoreline in the final. They had won the Sir Thomas Lipton Trophy, which some came to consider as the first World Cup.

Two years later, West were invited back. This time, a Swiss team consisting of players from Zurich was comfortably dispatched, before an Italy constructed of footballers from Juventus were annihilated 6-1. The team of miners had schooled them, as Connolly demonstrated via a contemporary press clipping from Italy: 'Now we must learn lessons from the higher level! After two years we have already learned two clear lessons. Let's hope we can make the best of them.'

West Auckland Town had won the 'World Cup' again, but in doing so starved club finances. Back home, they were forced to hand over the trophy to pay off a debt and by the Easter of 1912 had withdrawn from the Northern League.

Scripts often end that way in England's north-east, and the sequel's denouement was not much better – though they eventually got their trophy back, in 1994 it was burgled from the club's ground, never to be seen again. Although my loyalties this evening should have rested with the Teesside team, I could not help hoping that a new trophy would soon be swelling their cabinet.

The chemical scientists of Synthonia were blind to such romanticism. They forced themselves on their opponents from the off, swarming like wasps on a dropped 99 ice cream. Their bulky, brusque centre-forward Ian Ward wore a number 5 shirt. Perhaps he plotted to lull West Auckland's centre-halves into thinking that he was a member of their secret society, the villain spy in a false moustache. He harrumphed into aerial encounters and dislodged markers forcefully as if they were rotten teeth that must be pulled.

West responded by skimming across the field on the break, led often by their full-backs, Andre Bennett and Michael Hoganson.

Both players had arrived from professional academies having been released, in Hoganson's case after appearing in Derby County's first team. Indeed, of the 22 players who had started this evening's final, 13 had been signed to professional clubs, with a number starting games in the English Football League.

How far and fast they fall in this harsh terrain; one-minute Premier League dreams, and the next two-footed tackles in grounds with Portakabin changing rooms. By the end of the game, it was easy to detect which players had received this grounding by the way they ran, nudged the ball around with different parts of their feet to the others and begged more from the referee, often squealing to enforce their point. This split was emphasised later on when one of West's former professionals appeared to have been felled in the penalty area. 'Ha'way ref!' he implored. 'Ged up, man,' shouted a jaded Synners' voice. 'Every bleedin' time.'

Next to me stood a specimen from one of a football crowd's newest breed, the Master Analyst. Usually men in their twenties or early thirties, in recent years they had materialised with their confident talk of half-spaces and transitions. Applying Premier League principles to a stockpile of players who had spent the day plumbing or driving forklift trucks, he deplored how there was 'no football in there. No press. No movement.' A few minutes on, he began running through the faults of the entire Billingham team, and relating how dire they were at 'recycling possession.' 'Liam, man,' said one of his friends, 'you couldn't even get in the school team.'

With terraces knit tight to the pitch, at throw-ins the magnificence of Synners' shirts could be truly comprehended. Having been adopted or sustained more in rugby than football, quarter-colours are a rare curio, especially in traffic-light green. It added a hint of jester-like or clownish diversion, as if the referee might go to book a player but find his notebook and card had been replaced with a long and tedious string of colourful hankies. This slapstick impression was magnified when a cross fell towards forward Danny Chapman but he succeeded only in volleying the ball straight into teammate Kurtis Howes' face.

The first half was trickling by with hardly an effort on goal. After Synners' rampaging start, the pace of the game had slowed and rot had set in. As a sporting contest, the match now had all the joie de vivre of 5am on an airport tarmac transport bus. Enjoyment could be taken from listening to the petty squabbles between players ('I never touched yer, yer sack of shite') or observing trifling details like the outlandish size of West Auckland's shirt numbers. They seemed to be wearing a large-print version of regular digits, which looked like wrought iron house numbers on mansion gates.

Despite this dingy offering, though, dissent beyond the views of the Master Analyst was almost absent. It was clear that most people in the ground were soothed and satisfied by the mere fact of being here. Now they were back among the barks and the outraged howls, the snaps and pops of a football being struck, the idle chatter and the nonsense exhortations to 'Just flick it', the trains clattering by and the snack bar queue beginning to build. This was all we had waited for and all we asked. The match was, for now, secondary.

As if sensing our ambivalence and demanding our attention, in the last moments before the interval both teams cobbled together smithereens of attacking play. First, two of West Auckland's Middlesbrough Academy alumni combined, winger Liam Hegarty dribbling and then deftly finding Bennett, who shimmied and crossed with unerring accuracy. It appeared that for those 20 seconds, both had channelled their old potential, like a wizened piano maestro suddenly sobering up enough to play. Then an injury to Billingham's Ward removed him from the picture, allowing his team to attack on the ground and at pace, as if the teacher had left the classroom and his pupils were able to express themselves freely. They provoked a free-kick, which Howes curved with a rare brand of vim. It was saved, and half-time had the 0-0 it probably deserved.

West Auckland began the second period with great verve, as if they had been told it was 'next goal wins'. 'This is better,' barked their forward, Kyle Fryatt. Soon afterwards, he was fouled in the box but no penalty was given. This incensed a colony of West supporters, who for some time would now enjoy the forgotten dark pleasure of wallowing in injustice. Synners' keeper Daniel Dixon responded to the opposition's onslaught by issuing firmer and more frequent instructions to his defenders, and it occurred to me that most of what a goalkeeper shouts is aimed at ensuring the ball stays away from him. In his cries of 'Close him down' and 'Get it out', the keeper brings to mind an arachnophobic family member screaming 'Don't let that bloody spider near me'.

On winked the immaculate floodlights, industrial giraffes perfect against a flamingo sky. Perhaps West were blinded: their midfielder Arron Thompson sliced a clearance that levitated dangerously into the area, at which point his teammate Evan Horwood arrived to sweep up the danger but instead missed the ball entirely. It fell to Synners' Joseph Dixon. He could see his hands embracing that comely trophy. Instead, he cudgelled his shot into the stomach of a West Auckland defender, who writhed and whined with such force that he could be heard over a passing freight train. The ball stammered out for a goal-kick, which was then hit straight out of play. 'Eeee, I wish they'd lock these buggers down again,' said a man behind me.

Then, with 20 minutes remaining, a marvel and a freakish extravagance: somebody scored a goal. The man to break this game's spell of ineptitude was Anthony Bell, whose snapshot struck a Synners defender and hooped its way above goalkeeper Dixon and into the net. West cheers floated across the ground. They had more followers here than had been apparent. Now, each of them felt outed and emboldened, their camouflage shed. They were all Spartacus and they had come to win the cup.

Billingham searched for an equaliser but seemed to fumble forward rather than launch any concerted line of attack. At times they seemed confused by what was happening, displaying the kind of bafflement and dizziness usually brought on by walking up a static escalator. Instead, just as the game was set to end, West

Auckland wrestled free of the quagmire and scored again through Fryatt. The whole team celebrated, and a resonant, sustained cheer that the men of 1909 and 1911 would have been humbled by flew from the mouths of travellers in yellow and black scarves. 'Ah well. It's just nice to get out,' said a Synners man to my right. 'Aye,' replied his friend. 'They are cheating bastards, though.'

As waddling men from the Durham FA prepared the trophy and medals, I wandered behind the opposite goal and towards the gate. In one corner, a bus shelter had been repurposed as a small stand. Its timetables were still displayed; underneath this very Perspex, people had waited for the 6, the 21A, the 58, the 558 and the 565. A sign announced its removal from Stockton town centre, in November 2013, as part of regeneration works on the High Street. I smiled and said thank you to the sky that the reviving, eccentric world of football was once more there for us.

On the train back north from Billingham, a young boy, his dad and his grandad sat around a table. They had been at the game. Dad asked son who his favourite player was. Grandad carefully filed his matchday programme into a plastic wallet, then closed his eyes and nodded off with a smile on his face. It felt like there was a future again.

EPILOGUE

Three months later, the days we had dreamed of arrived. Almost a year-and-a-half after football fell silent, in August 2021 our grounds would be open to capacity. It was only when walking towards them did we finally, truly believe that we were going home and staying there.

Blending into the shoal striding towards the Riverside for Middlesbrough's first game back there, I was struck by the happy look of possession in people's eyes. All were moths to the flame. They stared intently ahead; if they looked away, it might disappear. Thousands bounced along, a red tide that turned August into a festive procession. We queued rowdily, like boisterous, butterfly-stomached children outside a theme park. Grown men hopped up and down. Some closed their eyes disbelievingly. A woman in her early twenties rattled her hands on a metal door and hollered: 'I'm going back!' It was her moment, and yet we all felt the same – an entirely personal, completely shared point in time.

Soon, each of us walked out of the darkness and into the light. The turf seemed more luminous and immaculate than it had for years. As the teams sauntered on, there was noise enough to wake the man in the moon. A huge banner was raised in the South Stand: 'This Is Our Way Of Life', it averred simply and poignantly. And now that way of life was returning, as if a despotic leader had been expelled.

In front of us, a man reached one arm around a friend's shoulder and gestured towards the pitch with the other, as if he were a gameshow host revealing answers and prizes to a contestant. I looked around and saw fathers and sons and mothers and daughters standing in shared, contented silence, all with lost and smiling eyes. At one time, we had felt bereft; here was the resurrection.

The following Saturday, craving more of this renaissance, I visited Victoria Park for Hartlepool United's fixture with Walsall. Pools had already played two home games, but August matches had retained a newness; this was a honeymoon period. Even results did not yet matter as they once had. Outside, travelling Saddlers fans dismounted their supporters' club coaches, rubbed their hands together and cried 'You rrrreds' into the air. In all my thoughts of pining for our homes, I had neglected the heady splendour of an away day. The fixture list suddenly doubled in size.

'You can stick your fucking drummer up your arse' sang those visitors once they were inside the ground, a retort to the thumped beats arising from a pocket of young Poolie ultras. There would be no new age of kindness and consideration on the terraces, no peace ushered in after the shared darkness. Not many of us would have it any other way. Ditto early in the game, when a Walsall player tried to trap a pass but saw it run under his foot and out of play. There was no sympathy or shouts of 'hard lines'; instead, thousands heckled uproariously. It seemed as though supporters had missed schadenfreude as much as they had missed good play or goals.

In the paddock alongside the pitch, small groups of men in their sixties and seventies grumbled in satisfied, told-you-so voices when it was Pools' turn to give the ball away. Football grounds remained arenas for offloading all kinds of emotions. A man walked along the gangway at the front, staring so lovingly at his tray of chips that he almost tripped over. There was something seductive about these odd, often poor quality, mid-afternoon matchday meals that had made us pine for them. Behind the goal, terrace dwellers looked forward as one and probably shared the same thoughts through each twist and movement on the pitch. All those here and in every ground felt gratitude: their team had welcomed them back and for the first time in aeons made Saturdays *count*. They were also capable of making that day soar – goals raised a pleased bunch to jubilation. Here, Hartlepool's Tyler Burey went on a run that had noise spreading along the paddock as in the crescendo of a horse race. He then speared the ball into the top corner. How they roared and how they hugged. Next to me, a dad and his grown-up daughter suddenly reversed 30 years in time and she seemed to shrink in his arms.

Hartlepool went on to win 2-0. Towards the end, seagulls had circled above menacingly. This time, they would be fed. The crowd left in stages, just like they always had – the elderly and the limping first, then the dads dashing to beat the traffic and pulling along kids who looked back and watched the game over their shoulders, and then the pot-bellied with a thirst on. Those many who stayed saluted their team as if they were heading off to sea. Neil Diamond's 'Sweet Caroline' infused the air with more glad tidings and, in shuffled steps, supporters made for their other homes.

That song had, improbably, become the anthem of the England national team's run to the final of Euro 2020, a competition belatedly staged across this continent during June and July. At Wembley, Hampden Park and on foreign shores, supporters had returned to those matches in increasing numbers as the competition progressed. Perhaps, during football's oddest era, we had lost all objective sense of what a good tournament was, but many revelled in the fine play and high times of this edition. Here, it helped that three home nations – Scotland and Wales alongside England – had qualified.

More than that, though, Euro 2020 acted as a reminder of the universality of football and how our love was shared everywhere. With foreign travel often closed down, and difficult when permitted, after more than a year of isolation our sport burned borders and reminded us that this wonderful, maddening pursuit belonged to all people. Off the field and on it, in their persistent anti-racist action of taking the knee, England's likeable squad excelled morally. The same could not be said of all their supporters; before and during the final at Wembley, many thousands acted with a cowardly form of aggression and violence that had absolutely nothing to do with the supporting life most of us had so dearly missed.

Thinking backwards through my journey, tracing the lines from Easter Road to Workington, and Jarrow to Southport, the tenacity and resilience of our love for the game stood out. It was there at the fence in Galashiels, there in the volunteers catching lotto tickets in Lancaster or double-underlining signs in Billingham, and there in the songs of Kendal ultras and the tenses of Northumbrian goalkeepers. We have a dense sense of loyalty to this sport and our teams. It is an enduring affection that had now overcome its greatest peril for many years. That endurance demonstrated the very best of people – their humour, creativity and ability to hang tight to hope in the bleakest days.

The volatile 2020/21 season reaffirmed the meaning and importance of football to people. Though a frippery when placed in the context of hellish ICU wards and harrowing Covid statistics, in its own right and to us, it mattered more than ever. We should never be embarrassed about that.

It was a remarkable season. May there never be another like it.

SELECTED BIBLIOGRAPHY

Bill Shankly: It's Much More Important Than That by Stephen F. Kelly (Virgin Books, 1997).

Hillmen: A History of Football in Coquetdale by Jon Tait (Rough Badger Press, 2017).

Leeds United and Don Revie by Eric Thornton (Robert Hale Ltd, 1970).

Oxford Dictionary of National Biography (via oxforddnb.com).

Revie: Revered and Reviled by Richard Sutcliffe (Great Northern, 2010).

Secret Kendal by Andrew Graham Stables (Amberley Publishing, 2017).

Secret Southport by Jack Smith (Amberley Publishing, 2017).

Shankly by Bill Shankly (Barker, 1976).

Shanks: The Authorised Biography of Bill Shankly by Dave Bowler (Orion, 2013).

So Sad, So Very Sad . . . The League History of Workington AFC: Part One by Martin Wingfield (Worthing Typesetting, 1991).

Soccer's Happy Wanderer by Don Revie (Museum Press, 1955).

Southport History Tour by Hugh Hollinghurst (Amberley Publishing, 2019).

The Miners' Triumph: The First English World Cup Win in Football History by Martin Connolly (Oakleaf Publishing, 2018).

The Sandgrounders: The Complete League History of Southport F.C. by Geoff Wilde & Michael Braham (Palatine, 1995).

www.cumbria-industries.org.uk.

www.rothburyfc.com.

ACKNOWLEDGEMENTS

Immense thanks to Charlotte Croft, Publisher at Bloomsbury, for commissioning another of my books and making many a brilliant editing and creative suggestion. Her colleagues Sarah Skipper, Zoë Blanc and Robert Sharman were a pleasure to work with, and the copy editing of Jenni Davis and eagle-eyed proofreading of Richard Whitehead very much appreciated. I am again grateful to my agent David Luxton and his colleague Rebecca Winfield for their work and support.

I am always indebted to local and football historians as reflected in the bibliography, with a special mention for Dan Hayes at Southport FC. Thanks too go to the following media and administrative staff at various clubs: Craig Brown (Dunfermline), Debi Ritchie (Gala Fairydean Rovers), Dianne Blair (Cowdenbeath), Kenny Millar (Hibernian) and Rab More (Raith Rovers). Some words and ideas in this book were adapted and developed from pieces of mine previously published in *Nutmeg* magazine.

The backing and love of my parents and sisters is always within me, spurring me on, and I have very much enjoyed reading lines to Homer the cat this time, much to his annoyance. Above all else, though, heartfelt, deepest thanks to Marisa and Kaitlyn. They are always there in the great dugout of life, offering encouragement and occasionally barking useful tactical instructions. And, yes, our lass: you came up with the book title. Your cheque is in the post.